Crash Course in Time Management for Library Staff

Recent Titles in Libraries Unlimited
Crash Course Series

Crash Course in Time Management for Library Staff

Brenda Hough

Crash Course

An Imprint of ABC-CLIO, LLC

Santa Barbara, California • Denver, Colorado

Library of Congress Cataloging in Publication Control Number: 2017046406

ISBN: 978-1-4408-5067-7 (paperback)
        978-1-4408-5068-4 (ebook)

22   21   20   19   18   1   2   3   4   5

This book is also available as an eBook.

Libraries Unlimited
An Imprint of ABC-CLIO, LLC

ABC-CLIO, LLC
130 Cremona Drive, P.O. Box 1911
Santa Barbara, California 93116-1911
www.abc-clio.com

This book is printed on acid-free paper ∞

Manufactured in the United States of America

This book is dedicated to several people.

First of all, thank you to Lisa Barnhart and Mary Ross. This book would not exist if they had not first helped me create a course on the topic in 2012.

Next I would like to dedicate this book to moms and dads everywhere. I see you there, juggling and worrying and making things work, and you are amazing.

And finally, I express my love and thanks to my husband and son. To borrow from a Raymond Carver poem, what I want in this life is "to call myself beloved, to feel myself beloved on the earth." Because of you, Fred and Beckett, I do.

CONTENTS

PREFACE

While I have probably always been a bit overly fond of my daily planner, my interest in time management turned to near obsession after my son was born. As I juggled the various roles I was playing in my personal and professional lives, it became clear that managing time was more than my time, but it involved the people around me. In my quest to manage projects and hours more effectively and gracefully, I not only discovered useful tools and strategies, but I also discovered that it was surprisingly fun to talk to other people about time management. Since that time, I have been presenting time management tools to audiences at conferences, workshops, and most recently for in a popular four-week course for Infopeople. This book introduces tools, hints, explanations, and suggestions to you, while encouraging you to pick and choose and devise a system that makes sense for you and your life.

Chapter 1 introduces how to streamline your processes to become more effective. When you are more effective in the workplace, you feel on top of things rather than overwhelmed. In reality, it's not really time management that matters as much as energy management. Being aware of our energy levels and aware of our capacity can lead to success in managing our time.

We learned to tell time at a very early age, watching the classroom clock carefully as those hands moved to the magic time of recess and lunch and dismissal for the day. We learn the months of the year and the days of the week, but beyond those basic building blocks of time measurement, many of us never received formal training in time management.

Chapter 2 introduces time logs and suggests keeping one at least for a short period of time. Tracking your time allows you to learn to realistically assess your actual usage of time. This can be done with pen and paper or with online tools. By analyzing a time log, you discover what you are actually doing so that you can determine and eliminate your potential time wasters.

Setting goals and priorities in both your professional and personal life is discussed in Chapter 3. When did you last sit down to identify your top priorities at work and outside the workplace? What matters most to you? Do the activities that fill the time log that you completed in Chapter 2 match your priorities?

What if you aren't doing what you *want* to be doing? What if the way you spend your time doesn't match your priority list? If there's a big disconnect between your priorities and your time usage, then you will always struggle with how you are using your time. You may be quite efficient but you may not feel happiness or a sense of accomplishment. This chapter helps you take a realistic look at your present goals and priorities can help you recognize ways in which your time does not match up with what is important to you. Before you end this chapter, you will rethink your goals and priorities, and, if necessary, set new ones.

Chapter 4 introduces you to some very basic tools for time management beginning with how to create a "to-do" list both on pen and paper or online. Here is where you note the activities that are in the near and distant future, those things which you are responsible for doing or seeing that they are done.

Keeping a calendar is probably the most basic time management tool of all. It helps you make sure you don't miss a dental appointment, a team meeting, or the deadline for a grant proposal. Scheduling requires an awareness of when one can plan an event or hold a meeting.

In the book's discussion of time management strategies, the use of a timer is suggested for some tasks to help encourage focus. Setting the timer means working on the project for a specified length of time and then stopping with a return later.

The use of these tools is also helpful in learning to form helpful habits. What activities in your life can you make routine, so that you don't really even have to think about them?

Chapter 5 involves "Getting Past Procrastination." Calendars and schedules outline what needs to be done, but things can slide for a variety of reasons. We may avoid a boring task or put off one that we're uncertain about how to begin.

Large projects may seem overwhelming and the desire to put off starting the task seems preferable to plunging right into step one. Or sometimes when a project is coming to an end, the final stages can be stressful causing you to want to set it aside. Or, perhaps you said "yes" once too often and you have too many things on your to-do list or you underestimated how much time any of your other tasks might take.

Getting over the desire for perfection is the focus of Chapter 6. Do you try too hard to be perfect in everything you do or do you expect perfection in others? Perfectionism can lead to burnout, an inability to start a project, stress, or an unwillingness to take risks or even complete tasks. This chapter explains the difference between excellence and perfectionism. It also encourages recognizing that there are times when striving for efficiency rather than perfection makes the most sense.

Chapter 7 deals with distractions and interruptions, which are frequently cited challenges in library work environments. Whether it's that "ding" you hear every time a new e-mail arrives, coworker conversations near your desk, social media, or loud noises as construction takes place, distractions and interruptions must be addressed or at least accounted for in your estimates and goals for using your time. They must be dealt with or your to-do list for the day will not have many items marked complete.

Worksheets to use to help you identify your time management challenges and devise plans for being more effective are scattered throughout the book. You can enter your information and experiences, customizing an approach that makes sense for you. Ultimately, time management is a very individual thing and we need to be willing to experiment and learn. The good news is, time management can be learned. It's not an innate ability that some people have and others do not. Effective time management is a capability we all have within our reach.

CHAPTER 1

Introduction to Time Management

Almost everyone seems to feel busy. Even young children are rushed from activity to activity by harried parents trying to fit everything in. Social media posts lead us to believe that everyone else is doing so much (traveling, eating, exercising) that we feel pressure to keep up. In our workplaces, expectations seem to grow as resources shrink. Time management is a critical skill and one that cannot be ignored. But, how does one learn to manage that precious commodity, time?

An Amazon search for "time management" results in almost 30,000 titles, each promising secrets, tips, hacks, or systems that will lead to stress-free productivity. Dozens of new books and numerous articles about time management are written each year, so why create this book targeting library staff? Are the time management needs and challenges faced by those working in libraries unique? The answer to that question is both yes and no.

Techniques and tools that work in other professions often also work for people working in libraries. Clocks, calendars, and to-do lists are the basic building blocks of any time management system, and resources that are not library specific will be referenced throughout this book because they are helpful, and they can be tailored to fit the needs of library staff. For example, David Allen's *Getting Things Done* provides a variety of methods for moving tasks and projects out of your head and into a simple task management system. How a busy person breaks them into actionable items will be introduced in Chapter 4.

It is an example of an approach that has worked well for people in many professions, from teachers to business owners.

As I talk to library staff from organizations both big and small, I hear concerns and challenges that are not entirely the same as those faced by the people with office or desk-based jobs who are the target audience for most time management writing. In a library, someone may need to flow from delivering a story time to working on a grant proposal to fixing a printer jam to listening to a favorite patron's stories about his grandson's visit—all within the space of an hour.

Since the work environment in a library is different, the time management strategies that will work are different, too. Whether you are a new manager or a new parent or have been in your position for 15 years, it is not possible to make more time, but it *is* possible to make big improvements in your productivity and in your level of satisfaction with work and with life. This book is designed to help you develop those strategies.

WHY LEARN ABOUT TIME MANAGEMENT?

We can't make more time, but we can learn how to more effectively manage the time that we have available to us. Picture the White Rabbit in Lewis Carroll's *Alice in Wonderland*, as he frantically runs around holding a pocket watch and exclaiming, "I'm late, I'm late, for a very important date!" The anxiety he feels about a shortage of time is a common emotion in our contemporary world. Pay attention to the way people speak about time and you will probably be surprised to notice how frequently busyness comes up. When speaking to a friend on the phone and asking, "How are things going?" it's likely that friend will reply, "I've been so busy." When someone asks, "How are things at the library?" it's likely that an accurate response is "Things have been so busy!" While being busy is not bad, there are negative consequences to an ongoing overworked lifestyle. The sense of being overworked causes stress and stress can negatively impact both our health and our sense of well-being. Although some may feel that people working in libraries live a stress-free life reading books and magazines and telling stories to children, we know that is not an accurate picture.

This is a book written for people working in libraries and the purpose is not to help you streamline your processes so you can sell more widgets. The goal is a very human-centered focus on both individual well-being and on the important work you are doing in your organization and in your community so that you can continue to provide these critical services. People are not robots and in focusing on humans in the workplace terms like "higher productivity" and "streamlined processes" need to be cautiously considered. Effective time management is not about being a faster machine. Rather, it is about feeling less stress and greater satisfaction with work and life after work with friends and family. It is about feeling like you are making the best use of your time while you are in the workplace as you focus on meeting the needs of the community your library serves.

Changes in time management strategies are not always about "doing more" or doing things faster. In Chapter 2, you will track your time usage to record what you are actually doing. Sometimes the activities and reflection about how you are accomplishing them will lead you to realize that what you are trying to achieve is just not possible no matter how sophisticated your time management system is. As you take a close, realistic look at your time usage, you may realize that there is just not enough time in any day to do everything that you want or think that you need to do. This creates some questions you need to ask yourself:

Are you being asked to do too much? Or are you expecting too much from yourself? Is your supervisor underestimating the time it takes to accomplish a task? Does a colleague seem to be able complete one task faster because she or he has regular experience in carrying out that task?

On the other hand, do you sometimes underestimate, thinking you can accomplish a task in a shorter number of minutes? If you constantly try to complete in a time frame that doesn't account for the interruptions that might occur, then you are setting yourself up for stress and a sense of failure.

The tools described in this book can help you uncover these sorts of challenges, giving you the data and encouragement you need to push back by asking for more assistance or by finding ways to shift responsibilities. You may be inspired to talk to others about their time management strategies, sometimes discovering ways to get a job done more quickly or efficiently. Tracking your time will give you a more accurate view of how much time any task takes.

As he tracked his time usage, an experienced branch manager was surprised to realize how little focused time he really had available for projects and paperwork such as reports. Most of his time was spent in meetings, covering for staff, and addressing day-to-day issues that would arise. A children's librarian who was asked to prepare a brief presentation for the board summarizing highlights from the summer reading program was shocked to realize that it took over five total hours to prepare.

People choose to learn about time management for many reasons. For some, it is driven by fatigue, stress or overwork, but that is not always the reason. Some people are drawn to the topic because they want to do more. They long to be more creative or innovative but feel unable to find the time or energy in their days to do things that are beyond their normal routine.

While time management and innovation may at first glance seem disconnected, they are in fact related. Time management supports innovation. By identifying and eliminating distractions, for example, you can free up time to focus on creative endeavors. By being more focused and organized, you can not only find the time for coming up with new ideas, but you will have the discipline to put those ideas into action.

If you are a manager or director reading this book, you may need to learn how to help your staff see that it is OK to spend time on things like learning new things and developing innovative ideas.

For example, a number of libraries have started to implement weekly time allotments for staff to spend on learning or innovation. One example is at the Tooele City Library in Utah where director Jami Carter implemented a self-directed achievement program, and each staff member was asked to set one training goal each week that would be achievable in one hour. Creating the time and giving staff permission to use the time was the first step in a more innovative organizational culture.

IS TIME MANAGEMENT SOMETHING YOU CAN LEARN?

Culturally, we are socialized by the clock and it shapes our days. In kindergarten, or maybe even before, we start to learn to tell time. Adults use watches and timers and calendars to fill in the hours and days of the week and month. However, we remain likely to use a timer to make sure we don't overcook our boiled egg. However, the ability to measure time is a basic skill that we are taught as early as possible and we become adept at measuring time. However, managing time is different from measuring it.

Time *management*, as opposed to time *measurement*, is about planning and organizing how you spend your time. We know we cannot stop time. We cannot add more hours to the day. But what we can do is attempt to thoughtfully control how we spend our hours. We can identify and prioritize the tasks that we need to complete and then create a schedule for accomplishing those tasks. As you work through this book, you will assess your current time usage, identifying your priorities and also your challenges.

While discussed earlier, time measurement is a core competency taught in elementary schools, time management instruction is not as standardized. In college, you may have attended a study skills workshop that included time management strategies to help you be more successful in your studies. Your parents may have modeled effective time management techniques. A mentor may have given advice about goal setting and task prioritization. In large part, however, many of us are piecing together our approach without this type of direction and guidance.

Some people seem to be naturally better at time management than others. Some people are recognized as experts and have had stories and even have had films made about the topic. The classic book *Cheaper by the Dozen* detailed the lives of the Gilbreth family whose parents were time management experts. Made into a film in 1950, one learns how to survive with a family of 12 using time management techniques. Most of us do not have a family of 12 to manage, but we each have different personality characteristics, and we have had very different types of parental influence and various other nature and nurture dynamics shaping our methods and attitudes. While effective time management may seem to come more easily for some than it does for others, everyone can improve their abilities. Time management is something that you can learn. If you are willing to honestly assess your current situation and experiment with different tools and techniques, then you can make impactful changes.

IT'S NOT JUST TIME; ENERGY MATTERS, TOO

It is important to note that time management is not all about minutes and hours. Of equal or perhaps greater importance is energy. Just as hours in the day are limited, our capacity and energy levels are limited, too. While it is much more difficult to measure energy than time, gaining a greater understanding of our own energy limits is a powerful thing.

Effective time management requires realistic assessments of the energy tasks will require and the energy we have available. Not only do we need to know how much energy we have to use, but we also need to be focused on finding ways to replenish our energy with breaks, relaxation and vacations. When you are also focused on energy and not only on time, then you discover that half an hour spent taking a walk during your lunch break could result in greater productivity. When faced with a large task, getting up and away from my computer now and then to take a short walk or just free my brain often results in better work outcomes when I return than if I had just stayed at my desk with no break.

When focused on energy rather than time, it is impossible to focus only on work hours. It requires a holistic approach that extends beyond work hours and duties to include things like diet, sleep, and overall stress levels. The importance of emotions also cannot be underestimated. When dealing with too many demands on our time or with stressful challenges, we can become cranky, anxious, and our energy levels and time management are not nearly as effective. Confronting our time management issues may require addressing some of these negative emotions.

OUR MANAGEMENT OF TIME IS HIGHLY INDIVIDUAL

You do not need to have seen the movie *The Godfather* to know that one of its most frequently quoted lines is, "It's not personal. It's business." If you reverse that statement, you have an assertion that applies to time management: "It's not business. It's personal." Even if your time management goals start out completely work related, there is no way to explore this topic without taking a holistic look at how you are using all of your time and how you want to be using your time.

Our perceptions, strategies and feelings about time are subjective. While there are plenty of books and methods that promise to be *the* answer to your time management woes, it really is not a one-size-fits-all thing. Tracking time usage and becoming aware of time wasters may be a game changer for certain people, while using a timer for focused periods of work will work for others. A bullet journal may be life-changing for your friend but may not be a good fit for you at all. This book seeks to help you devise the systems and plan that will work uniquely well for you.

It is very likely that two people doing the same job will not manage their time in the same way. Carolyn is a technical services assistant at Library A and her workspace, workflows, and daily routines are different than Laura, who is a technical services assistant at Library B. Although their job duties are similar, the structure around their work is different.

Our individual circumstances impact the time management strategies that work for us. It is ill-advised to make assumptions or judgments about how other people spend their time without better understanding their perspective and circumstances.

Significant cultural differences exist and impact time management. Research time and cultures around the world and you will discover that there are essential differences in perceptions of time. Some cultures emphasize long-term thinking, while others are focused on the short term. Strict adherence to schedules is important in some cultures, while others are more flexible. For example, researchers have found that some cultures may have a monochronic orientation to time, while other cultures have a polychronic orientation. In a monochronic culture, time is money and a schedule is strictly adhered to. In a polychronic society, however, time is more fluid and the focus is on relationships, rather than the clock. An in-depth exploration of these cultural differences is beyond the scope of this book, but it demonstrates that our usage of time is a complex topic and we need to accept another's orientation. If we look at cultural differences related to time, it becomes even clearer that time is merely a construct. There is not one right way to manage time.

Believe it or not, time and time management are fascinating topics of conversation. Ask your friends, family members, coworkers and fellow dinner party guests how they manage their time and you will be surprised at the variety in responses. Even if you start with lighter questions, such as, *What apps do you use? or How do you keep track of to-dos?* you will find that almost any discussion about time quickly shifts to richer conversations about the things that matter to us most. At a recent workshop, I asked participants to talk to their tablemates about calendars, asking one another questions such as: *How many calendars do you use? Do you use a digital or a print calendar? What level of detail do you include in your calendar(s)?* People with one calendar were surprised to learn that some people maintain several (one woman in the workshop said she uses 6 (!) calendars for different purposes including one for work, one for her kids, one for her personal schedule, one for food and meal planning, etc.).

Discovering what works best for you is an ongoing process and as things change, your time management strategies will need to change, too. In the final chapter of this book, we will focus on creating a personalized plan for time management and ongoing time management learning. We begin with attitudes about busyness.

ATTITUDES ABOUT BUSYNESS

Imagine two people who work at a library: Kate and Linda. Kate is incredibly busy and never takes vacations. Contrarily Linda seems to comfortably accomplish the things she needs to complete in her work day and she take breaks and vacations regularly, too. Based upon these brief descriptions, what is your perception of these individuals? Who do you think has a higher status? If you chose Kate, you are not alone. Studies have shown that people tend to associate busyness with higher status.

When being busy is linked to being important and in demand, you may think you need to plan your work so that you will always be busy. Part of the work you need to do when striving to make changes is your time management strategies is to address your attitudes about busyness.

What are your perceptions of busyness? Is being "so busy" a status symbol for you? What do you think of someone who is able to get work done quickly and has time for relaxation? Have you ever considered the level of difficulty of any work that a colleague appears to do quickly? Do you skip lunch and breaks? Do you use your vacation days? If you don't use your vacation days, why don't you?

I grew up with a workaholic father, and while I am thankful for the strong work ethic I developed under his influence, one of my biggest personal time management challenges is to understand the very real difference between being a hard worker and having an unhealthy focus on work. Workaholism is much more socially acceptable (even socially admired) than other addictions, yet it is a damaging force that prioritizes work over relationships and personal well-being. It is important to understand that vacations, breaks, and relaxation are good and necessary things. If you find yourself not being able to fully believe that, then you may want to spend some time exploring the impact family or societal messages have had on your outlook. It took visits from three ghosts to help Ebenezer Scrooge see the problems with his obsessive focus on work. There are easier ways to gain personal understanding and make changes.

CHANGE BEGETS CHANGE

Charles Dickens said, "Change begets change. Nothing propagates so fast." It is change that frequently leads us to a heightened interest in time management. A job promotion with greater responsibility, a new baby, a health issue that impacts energy levels—these are all examples of changes that can lead to our old time management strategies no longer working, requiring us to focus on finding new ways to do things. Somewhat counterintuitively, it is often change itself that drives us to want to make more changes.

For me, my intense interest in time management really started when my son was born. I had always been a list maker and an organized calendar keeper, but once my son was born I felt overwhelmed and pulled in different directions. My old time management attitudes and strategies were not adequate and I needed to up my game. Late night cram sessions were no longer an option, so I need to maximize the time I had available for work. I started using a time-tracking app to recognize where I was spending my time. I realized the importance of creating organizational systems that prevented me from wasting time redoing things I had already done or searching for information that I had already obtained.

Sometimes it is not the circumstances in our lives that have changed, but instead changes in the world around us that impact our time management. Consider, for example, smartphones. They have been part of most of our lives for a decade or less. Smartphones have impacted our time management in both positive and challenging ways. Ask people about the distractions in their lives and many will cite their phone, listing things like social media, scanning online news, or being in constant touch with contacts from our personal and professional lives. Yet smartphones also offer solutions that would not have been possible just 15 years ago, with apps for almost every need you can imagine. In this book, we'll talk about both the pros and the cons of smartphones, with strategies to try to address the distraction they provide and apps to try that help you structure and organize your time and tasks.

The simplest approach to change is to:

- Know where you *are.*
- Know where you *want to b*e.
- Make a plan to get from where you *are* to where you *want to be.*

The first part of this book is dedicated to helping you identify where you are, which is accomplished by looking at your current approaches to time management. Future chapters will help you define your priorities, identify where you want to be, and find tools that will assist you in getting there.

CHAPTER 1 KEY TAKEAWAYS

- Effective time management has many benefits. On a personal level, it can lead to decreased stress and increased satisfaction with life and work. These changes can lead to improved functioning in our jobs and better service for our communities.
- Effective time management can be learned.
- One size does not fit all. Our attitudes, preferences, and preferred approaches are highly individual. Cultural attitudes to time also differ significantly.
- Job or other life changes frequently spark a desire to gain new time management strategies.

In this chapter, you were introduced to time management as a topic that can be studied and learned. In the next chapter, you will start your time management learning journey by analyzing the ways in which you currently are spending your time. This awareness is key!

CHAPTER 2

How Do You Spend Your Time?

We each have 24 hours in a day. The desire for just a few more hours is alluring and we think, "*If only I had a couple of extra hours to focus on this . . .*" Fans of the *Harry Potter* series, however, may remember the lesson Hermione learned in her third year at Hogwarts. The ambitious Hermione wanted to attend more classes than time would allow so she used a Time-Turner to add extra hours to the day. Rather than enabling her to blissfully attend more classes and do more homework, the extra hours in the day left her exhausted and she ends up quitting a couple of the classes and turning the Time-Turner back in. As we discussed in Chapter 1, hours in the day are not the only consideration. Energy levels need to be considered, too. Making changes in our time management strategies first requires us to have a realistic assessment of how we are currently spending our time and energy.

THE WAYS WE SPEND OUR TIME

Laura Vanderkam is an author and a researcher who writes about time management. In her book *168 Hours*, she makes the point that everyone has 168 hours in a week. She encourages readers to keep a time log in order to think about their 168 hours and how they are choosing to use them. For example:

> If you work 40 hours per week, sleep 7 hours per night, spend 14 hours per week on meal preparation and eating, spend 12 hours per week on laundry and other household chores . . . you've quickly reached 115 hours. There are, however, still 53 remaining hours. How do you use them?

The United States Bureau of Labor Statistics conducts the ongoing American Time Use Survey, which measures the amount of time people spend doing various activities, such as work, childcare, housework, watching television, volunteering, and socializing. Data for the survey is collected by having participants complete a 24-hour time diary followed by a telephone interview during which they are asked about the survey. The data captured provides a fascinating lens through which we can look at American life. For example, according to recent American Time Use Survey data, time spent reading for personal interest and playing games or using a computer for leisure varied greatly by age. Individuals age 75 and over averaged 1.1 hours of reading per weekend day and 20 minutes playing games or using a computer for leisure. Conversely, individuals ages 15 to 19 read for an average of 8 minutes per weekend day and spent 1.3 hours playing games or using a computer for leisure. Looking at this averaged data is interesting. Thinking about and learning about our own usage can be informed by noting how we are the same or different than these national averages. Data specifically focused on people who work in libraries would be particularly interesting. However, looking at national and professional averages is only useful to a point. We are all unique and our time management is highly individualized. Keeping our own time log can be particularly useful when starting a journey to better time management.

Is it really necessary to keep a time log? Don't we each already have a good idea of the ways in which we spend our time? Research actually shows that we are notoriously bad at estimating how much time we spend doing things. The 9 precious minutes of sleep pressing the snooze button gives us in the morning seems to fly by, while waiting for 10 minutes in line at the Department of Motor Vehicles can feel like an eternity. And who hasn't experienced the blissful feeling of losing our sense of time as we read a really good book or listen to a piece of music? Keeping a time log can help us have data to back up our personal perceptions.

HOW TO KEEP A TIME LOG

Most of us have had (or currently have) jobs that require us to "punch the clock," whether we manually put a card into a machine to record the times we arrive and leave work or whether we simply are using "punch the clock" as an idiom to describe the act of going to work. Logging time is not something unheard of in the library profession. Every summer children around the country log the hours they spend reading as part of their participation in summer reading programs.

Using a time log for three or more days will help you to gain a deeper understanding of your own time usage. Ongoing usage of a time log leads to even higher levels of understanding. Jot down (or enter text into the log on your computer, tablet, or phone) noting your activities during a day. For example, a typical start to a day may look like this:

6:30 AM	wake up, make/drink coffee, get dressed, etc.
7:00 AM	wake up son and focus on getting him fed, dressed, and ready for school
7:45 AM	drive son to school
8:00 AM	drop son off at school and drive to work
8:15 AM	handle work e-mails (write/reply)
9:00 AM	work on technology project
10:00 AM	meeting with strategic planning team

As you keep your log, in addition to noting the tasks, it is also useful to note as much detail as possible about the things that use your time. For example, if during the 9:00 AM–10:00 AM project work time you receive a phone call that lasts 5 minutes, make a note of that. If during the 45 minutes you spend on e-mail, a coworker stops by your desk to have a conversation that lasts 10 minutes, then make a note of that, too. Interruptions and distractions have an impact on your ability to effectively manage your time. We will talk about this more later in the book. It can also be useful to note your energy level or emotions around different activities. For example,

"10:00 AM–11:30 AM Worked on literacy program planning—really was in the zone!!" or
"3:00–3:30 Tried working on article for library newsletter, but was not feeling creative."

Depending upon your focus, you may want to keep a time log for work time only. You may want to keep a time log that covers both work and non-work time.

A time log can be as simple as a pen-and-paper worksheet with ½-hour slots for entries. A web search for "time log" will result in numerous free templates that can be downloaded or you can use the one in this book.

TIME LOG

Use this time log to track your activities and to note the date/time you start/complete a task.

Date	Time	Task

There are also plenty of technology tools that can help you track and analyze your time usage. Two popular tools that will be highlighted here are Toggl and RescueTime.

Toggl

Toggl (www.toggl.com) is a straightforward tool for logging time. Simply type text to describe, *What are you working on?* Set-up projects to categorize your entries. Click "Start" when you start working on the task and then "Stop" when you quit working on it. After you have been tracking your tasks for a while, then you can create a Summary Report to see how much time you have spent on each project.

Both a free version of Toggl and a "Pro" version with a fee are available. For most people working in libraries, the free version will be adequate. You can use Toggl as an individual or it can be set up for use by a team, too. Note that teams with over five members will need to use the Pro version. You can use Toggl on your desktop computer (Windows, Mac, or Linux) or on your Android or iOS devices, too.

Pros:

- Easy to use.
- Free version is usually adequate.
- Clean interface design.

Cons:

- Easy to forget to "start" and "stop" the timer when you begin or quit working on a task.
- Must have a device with you (either your desktop or smartphone) in order to track (or else you need to remember to manually enter time for offline tasks once you are back online). This can be a challenge for some library staff. For example, one woman noted, "I don't have a designated computer at work and signing in and out all the time seems overly intensive."
- If you don't want to track your time on an ongoing basis, it may not be worth the time required to set up projects and complete other fine-tuning of the tool.

See https://support.toggl.com/ to learn more.

RescueTime

RescueTime (www.rescuetime.com) is not a time log. Instead it is a time monitor. It runs in the background on your computer and mobile devices and monitors how you use them. How much time are you spending on Facebook? How much time do you devote to e-mail? Reports show the applications and websites you spent time using. You can set time usage goals for the day and RescueTime will let you know whether or not you achieved them.

There's a free version called RescueTime Lite and a Premium version with a fee, too. You can use RescueTime on your desktop computer (Windows, Mac, or Linux) or on your Android or iOS devices, too.

Pros:

- Easy to use.
- Automatically monitors activities so you don't need to remember to click start and stop.
- Gives you insight into where your time goes while you're on your computer or smartphone.

Cons:

- Many of the cool features are only available if you're using the Premium version.
- Only monitors tech use (although the Premium version allows you to manually enter offline activities, too).
- If you don't want to track your time on an ongoing basis, it may not be worth the time required to set up projects and complete other fine-tuning of the tool.

See https://www.rescuetime.com/ to learn more.

ANALYZING YOUR TIME LOG

After you have kept a log for a day or two, then you can analyze the logs to see how you are using your time. Several things can be worthwhile to note, including your energy levels, the amount of time various tasks actually take you, and how your actual time usage differs from your estimates. Let's take a look at five things your time logs may help you do.

Identify Your Work Flow

All of us know some people who do their best work in the morning, as well as others who are at their best in the afternoon or even during the nighttime hours. We also may know our own preferences and the natural rhythms that flow throughout our days. Becoming more aware of and using those rhythms to help you determine what type of work to do when can increase your productivity. If your ability to focus is strongest during the mid-morning hours (as it is for many people), that is a good time to work on projects that require more attention and higher brain power. If your ability to focus is lower in the afternoon, then that may be a better time to focus on tasks that require less attention.

A library manager discovered that she was spending her valuable highly productive time doing a routine task (handling the library's cash activities and going to the bank). After keeping a time log and considering her energy levels, she switched those to a different time of day, when she was less "in the zone" and better suited to less thoughtful activities. A technical services staff person said, "I became more aware of how much of a morning person I am and I will need to critically look at how I structure my days."

Get Real with Time Estimates

Being able to estimate time usage is an important skill. If you want to be able to accurately schedule your time, you need to know how long various projects are going to take. Yet our ability to estimate how long something will take is often unreliable. One library technology trainer said that when he started developing classes for the public, he drastically underestimated how long it would take:

> I was only giving myself an hour or two to plan an hour of instruction. I quickly realized that it took me a whole lot longer.

Being aware of and able to predict time usage requires tracking and attention and a whole lot of practice.

The billable hours model, which is frequently used by legal professionals, accountants, and freelance consultants, is not appropriate for most library work. Most of us do not charge for our services by the hour, but I encourage you to think like people who do. Imagine you had to bill someone for your hours. Imagine you had to estimate the amount of time a project would take you so that you could provide a potential client with a project cost. Thinking about time in that way helps create consciousness in a different way than during a typical eight to five work day. We often underestimate the amount of time tasks and projects will take. A time log can help us learn more and make more accurate estimates. One school librarian said keeping a time log helped her realize how long things take:

> I was surprised at how long it took me to complete what I always thought were simple tasks.

Conversely, keeping a time log can also help you realize that tasks that you dread actually take less time than you think. One library manager found:

> The time log helped me determine how much time is required to do regularly scheduled, rather lengthy tasks, i.e., monthly reports. As I was logging my days, I realized that I exaggerate when I think about the demand these tasks make on my schedule. I was pleasantly surprised to see that I was using less time than

I expected to finish some monthly reports. This took away some of my anxiety, which meant that I worked more quickly and efficiently on the task at hand instead of worrying about it.

Identify Time Wasters

One of the most important things tracking your time can help you do is to carefully assess ways in which you may be wasting time. We'll analyze this more in subsequent chapters, but for now, consider these potential time wasters and determine if any of them ring true for you.

- E-mail addiction: Many of us are caught in a flow that includes repeatedly checking our e-mail and changing our course of action in response to whatever appears in our in-box.
- Pursuit of perfection: Do you find it difficult to feel satisfied with the work you produce? Do you always have a sense that things could be better so you continue to work on them until they are due? Do you feel that you are forced to turn in work that is "imperfect"?
- Interruption zone: Do you work in a setting that makes it difficult to concentrate on a project long enough to complete it or make substantial progress on it? Are you constantly being interrupted and having to change course in response to the interruptions? After talking to many people who work in libraries after they have tried time logging, it's clear that finding uninterrupted time to work on projects is a big challenge. We'll talk about this more in Chapter 7.
- Social media: Facebook is not bad. Twitter is not bad. In fact, many of us have pages and accounts for our libraries and are using these tools to create important connections with our communities. However, many of us also lose time by browsing too long. As with e-mail, it's not the tool that is the enemy. It's how we approach it. One library staff member noted that she was surprised by how many different activities she was doing and how frequently she switched between activities, *"I realized that I check my e-mail or Facebook when I get bored."*
- Lack of organization: Would better organizational systems save you time? One librarian found that she really wants and needs to be more organized, *"I plan programming, which includes a lot of phone calls, e-mails, and research. I found that so much of my time is spent trying to find papers and information that I have misplaced."*

Identify Accomplishments

It's useful to identify time wasters in our time logs, but it's also common for library staff who fill out time logs to be pleasantly surprised to realize how much they actually get done. The director of a small rural library shared:

While it feels like I'm rushing around like a chicken with its head cut off sometimes, keeping the time log helped me see that I really do accomplish a lot in a day.

Being More Mindful

Most of us won't keep time logs on an ongoing basis. Keeping a time log for even a few days, however, can help us continue to be more mindful of our time usage. When reflecting on her experience of keeping a time long, one woman said:

> *"Sometimes, if I forgot to write a task down, I couldn't remember exactly what I had done. It helped me realize that I want to be more mindful of what I'm doing.*

Another librarian found logging helped with her awareness, too:

> *Being aware is really useful, I am prone to getting into autopilot and just zooming through my day and then getting to the end and thinking what did I do? Did I do what I needed to do?*

TIME LOG RESISTANCE

While some of you will be excited to get started with logging your time, others may be feeling reluctant. It can be difficult, when already feeling like you don't have enough time, to take time to keep a time log. In my experience, the effort is worth it. Just as finding the time for exercise gives us more energy, finding the time to keep a time log gives us a solid and realistic assessment of where we are, so we can determine how it differs from where we want to be.

Many people working in libraries are wearing numerous hats and it can feel like no days are *typical*. While keeping a log for an entire day for several days in a row may work for some people, it may not be a good fit for you. Make the process work for you. If it works better to log a day here or there, then do that. One librarian reported to me that he does not think he'll use time logging again for logging his "regular" time, but he does think he will use it for special projects in order to recognize how long they take.

You may worry that you will be self-conscious about your time usage since you're logging it so it won't be accurate. This is called the Hawthorne Effect and researchers are well aware of it. People change their behavior, simply because they are being studied. It's hard to avoid this in research and it's hard to avoid this when keeping time logs. Just remember that your logs are for you. If you're exercising more, reading to your children more, or being a better person in some other way because you are recording your time usage, you will know that as you analyze the logs. In fact, it may be a hint as to how you think you should be spending your time. Not wanting to need to write a new entry could keep you on task, too. As one librarian said:

> *Keeping a time log influenced my behavior. When I was working on a project, I was more likely to stay on task just so I didn't have to stop and enter a new activity on my phone.*

Here's a sample completed time log. The person who kept this log was somewhat surprised to see how much time was spent on email. She also realized how little time she had to devote to her current priority project (preparing a presentation for her library's staff day). She wants to incorporate exercise into her daily routine, but is struggling to see where it could fit.

Daily Time Log

Date: april 1

Time	Activity	Time	Activity
7:00 am	· breakfast	7:00 pm	dinner
7:30 am	· shower	7:30 pm	TV
8:00 am	· catch bus	8:00 pm	TV
8:30 am	· @ work – check email	8:30 pm	TV
9:00 am	· library opening routine	9:00 pm	TV
9:30 am	· more email	9:30 pm	read
10:00 am	· meeting with brand	10:00 pm	sleep
10:30 am	supervisor	10:30 pm	ZZZZ
11:00 am	· cover desk for	11:00 pm	
11:30 am	lunch breaks cover desk	11:30 pm	
12:00 pm		12:00 am	
12:30 pm	· eat sandwich at my desk while	12:30 am	
1:00 pm	· replying to emails	1:00 am	
1:30 pm	· work on presentation	1:30 am	
2:00 pm	for staff day	2:00 am	
2:30 pm	· replying to emails	2:30 am	
3:00 pm	· cover desk for	3:00 am	
3:30 pm	afternoon breaks	3:30 am	
4:00 pm	· phone call regarding technology upgrade plans	4:00 am	
4:30 pm		4:30 am	
5:00 pm	· more work on staff day presentation	5:00 am	
5:30 pm	· library closing	5:30 am	
6:00 pm	routine	6:00 am	
6:30 pm	catch bus home	6:30 am	

From *Crash Course in Time Management for Library Staff* by Brenda Hough. Santa Barbara, CA: Libraries Unlimited.

CHAPTER 2 KEY TAKEAWAYS

- Keep a time log and use what you learn to manage your time more effectively.
- Pen and paper logs work but technology tools like Toggl and RescueTime can be helpful, too.
- Use time logs to identify your work flow, take a realistic look at how long things take, identify time wasters, identify accomplishments, and be more mindful.
- You may feel some resistance to keeping a time log. Find ways to make the process work for you.

In this chapter, you have taken the important first step. You have gained awareness of your current time usage. This awareness is essential as you begin the process of change and improvement. In the next chapter, you will take a look at your current goals and priorities in order to identify ways in which your time does or does not match up with what is important to you.

CHAPTER 3

Goals and Priorities

This chapter will cover matching your goals and priorities to how you are spending your time. You can focus on your personal life, your professional life, or both. You will be analyzing the time logs you began in Chapter 2 for the assignments here in Chapter 3.

You can be managing your tasks quite effectively, meeting deadlines and doing what needs to be done, yet not feel like you are managing your time well. In this case, it may not be procrastination or lack of focus that is your real problem. If what you are doing is not what you *want* to be doing or is not a priority in your personal life or your professional position or for your employer, then you will always struggle with how you are using your time. It is possible to be quite efficient but not to feel happy or fulfilled. Taking a realistic look at your present goals and priorities can help you realize ways in which your time does not match up with what is important to you. At the close of the chapter, you will be able to rethink your goals and if necessary, set new ones.

REVIEWING YOUR CURRENT GOALS

Are you reading this book through a purely professional lens? Or are you taking a more holistic perspective and looking at time in both your personal and professional life? It is likely that you have short-term

CURRENT GOALS

Goals:	A. Personal or worklife?	B. Short term or long term?	C. High, medium, or low priority?

From *Crash Course in Time Management for Library Staff* by Brenda Hough. Santa Barbara, CA: Libraries Unlimited. Copyright © 2018.

and long-term goals. What do you want to accomplish this week? This month? This year? In five years? In ten years? Take a moment to review your current goals and enter them into this worksheet. After you have listed your goals, then go through and mark responses in columns A, B, C, and D. In column A, use a *P* or a *W* to indicate if it is a personal or a worklife goal. In column B, use an *S* or an *L* to indicate if it is a short-term (can be completed in the next month) or a long-term goal (will take more than a month). In column C, use an *H* or an *M* or an *L* to indicate whether the goal is a high, medium, or low priority. In other words, how important is it to you or how important is it to your employer?

Did you have trouble coming up with goals? Or did you need to create a second sheet so you could list them all? Goals can include your intentions, your plans, your targets, and your desired results. Short-term goals should include projects and activities that you intend to complete in the next few weeks or months. How much control do you have over your current workplace goal-setting? Do you have a supervisor who helps direct the goals for your position? Reviewing long-term goals for your professional life can include envisioning where you see yourself in five years, ten years, or at retirement. What are your long-term goals at work? Think about how happy you are doing what you are doing right now. Do you ever think about seeking another role in this setting or will you ever want to change your setting completely?

Did you include personal goals, too? You may want to read more, to exercise more, to take more time for relaxation. Reviewing goals for your personal life obviously involves considering the people in your life. If you have a partner and/or children, then goals may be shared or interdependent. Or you may be responsible for the care of aging parents so your goals include that.

Later in this chapter, you will compare your goals worksheet to the time logs you created in the previous chapter. This will be a useful activity to help you identify whether or not you are spending your time in the ways that matter most to you. Before we complete that comparison, however, let's look a bit more closely at the ways in which people spend their time.

HOW YOU ARE SPENDING YOUR TIME?

We hear a lot about work-life balance. What is a life well lived? Gallup scientists have identified five broad categories that are essential to most people:

1. Career well-being: how you occupy your time or simply liking what you do every day
2. Social well-being: having strong relationships and love in your life
3. Financial well-being: effectively managing your economic life
4. Physical well-being: having good health and enough energy to get things done on a daily basis

5.   Community well-being: the sense of engagement you have with the area where you live (http://www.gallup.com/businessjournal/152204/why-work-life-balance-isn-balanced.aspx)

Within these five broad categories, we each have specific things that matter to us. Our time management feels effective if we are able to focus on the things that are important for our well-being. When we create goals and prioritize our actions so that we are working toward those goals, we shift from being reactive to being proactive. This greater sense of control is what time management work is all about. According to Gallup, 66 percent of people are doing well in at least one of the five categories, but only 7 percent of people are thriving in all five areas. If a person is not doing well in any one of these well-being categories, it impacts our overall sense of well-being and influences our satisfaction with our daily lives. When we strengthen our well-being in any of the five categories, we will improve our attitudes about our lives.

Again, as you read this book and complete the activities, you may choose to focus on your work life or you may want to focus more broadly, looking at both your personal and professional life. If you are ready for major change in your life, you can think about goals and priorities from a broad long-term perspective. If you are not seeking major change, but are simply looking for ways to make what you are currently doing less stressful, then it can still be useful to take the time to really get clear about your shorter-term goals and priorities. Take a look at the goals you listed in the worksheet earlier in this chapter. How many of these five types of well-being are addressed in your goals? Do you see each type represented? Are there a large number of goals that are focused on one of the well-beings? This may be an indication that is focused on improving that well-being in your life.

ASSESS YOUR TIME USAGE

Now it's time to review the time log you kept in Chapter 2. How have you been spending your time? How many projects are you working on right now? Are you trying to work on too many things? What activities have been your focus? You may find it useful to actually start a list of the various activities that you see in your time logs.

Now go through your time log and your activity list, and ask yourself: *What do I want to keep doing? What do I want to do more? What do I want to change?* Note the connection (or lack of connection) between how you are spending your time and how you would like to be spending your time. When you are effectively managing your time, then the things you are doing align with what really matters to you. Doing this exercise helps you figure out what's important and what's a distraction. One seasoned library director told me she likes to categorize things as:

Do, delegate, or ditch.

Our energy level is dramatically influenced by our attitude about a situation. If the things you are doing are in alignment with your goals and priorities, then completing them will feel like time well spent. If you are in a job or situation that is not the right fit for you, no matter how many time management techniques and tools you use, you're always going to feel negatively about the use of your time. Jobs and situations that do not match up with who we want to be and what we want to be doing will always feel draining.

As you review your time logs, also consider the five types of well-being that were summarized earlier in this chapter. Are you spending time on each of those types of well-being? Is there a type or two that deserves more of your attention?

While logging your time, you were encouraged to pay attention not only to what task you were doing but also to your mental and physical energy. As you look at your time logs, it is useful to notice which tasks engage you more completely. What were you doing when time seemed to fly by? What were you doing when time seemed to drag slowly? Being aware of those things will help you as you work to identify your goals and priorities.

Goals and priorities help us be more disciplined in the way we spend our time. In the next chapter, we will focus on a common time management tool, the to-do list. As we discuss goals and priorities, however, also consider a list suggested by Jim Collins, author of *Good to Great*—the "stop doing" list. What can or should you stop doing? There is not enough time to do everything. Decisions must be made about what to do but also about what *not* to do. For example, I've talked to many newly promoted managers or directors who have a hard time leaving the duties from their previous position behind. A woman who was promoted from a technical services position to a managerial position realized that she was trying to do her old job, in addition to fulfilling her new responsibilities as a manager. Sometimes we need to take a brutally honest look at how we are spending our time to assess the things that we need to let go.

RETHINKING GOALS

What matters to you? What is most important to you? What do you want to accomplish? How do you want to spend your time and energy? Hopefully, your analysis of your time log and your activity list helped you identify things that you want to do. Based upon that, now set realistic (yet ambitious) goals. If you have a lot of things you want to do, then start by writing 25–30 possibilities and then narrowing that

Goals:	Resources needed: Time, money, and other support	Why are you doing this? What are the benefits that will be derived? What happens if you don't succeed?

list down to the top 5 or 6. You don't want to spread yourself too thin. Some of the goals you include in this worksheet will be goals that you included in your initial goal worksheet earlier in the chapter. As you review what is important to you and as you assessed your time logs, however, it is likely that your list of goals will be significantly revised. As you identify your goals, consider the resources that are available (money, time, support from other people, community resources, etc.) to support you achieving that goal. Think about *why* you want to achieve the goal. What are the benefits? What will happen if you don't achieve the goal? Setting and working toward goals are skills that can be learned and in this section, the focus is on how to do that.

Make Your Goals SMART

You may have encountered the SMART goals acronym before. It's a useful way to approach writing goals that are clear and specific.

- **Specific**. Don't write a goal that is too general (like "Get more exercise."). Instead, make the goal as detailed and defined as possible. Write the goal in a way that articulates why it is important to you. ("Improve my health and feel stronger by exercising three times per week.")
- **Measurable**. You need to be able to measure whether or not you have achieved the goal. When you write goals that are measurable, then you will also be able to track your progress along the way. ("During this entire year, I will run three times per week at least 2 miles per run.")
- **Attainable**. The best goals are realistic yet ambitious. You want to stretch yourself and do new things but also consider restraints. Do you have the resources needed to attain the goal? Or can you obtain the needed resources? Is it a goal that you can realistically achieve with hard work and focus?
- **Relevant**. Goals should be meaningful and worthwhile. If you're writing a professional goal, then it often makes sense to connect them to your organization's goals and strategies, too. It's best to focus on goals that match up with other efforts and identified needs.
- **Time-bound**. Set dates for your goal. Things seem to happen when we attach deadlines and milestones. If you set a goal but do not set deadlines then it's likely to remain a fuzzy possibility in the future rather than a reality. If it's a large goal that will take weeks, months or even years, then set not only a target date for achieving the final goal but also set target dates and milestones along the way.

Review the goals you are writing to see if they are SMART. Doing so can help you set goals that will be achieved.

More Goal-Writing Tips

Identifying your goals and the resources it will take to achieve them is an essential part of being an effective time manager. Without clear focus and direction, it will be difficult to feel you are successfully managing your time. Here are more tips to help you create goals that are meaningful and appropriate for you.

- **Set short- and long-term goals.** How long would each of your goals take to accomplish? Set both short- and long-term goals. What would you like to achieve in the next six months? In the next six weeks? What can you accomplish today? If, for example, your goal is to makeover the staff lounge so it is more comfortable and inviting, then that is the long-term goal, which you will complete by the end of three months. There are many short-term goals that you can set now to move you toward that larger goal. You may want to solicit initial ideas from other staff for the next two weeks. You have a friend who is an interior decorator and she has agreed to take a look at the space to give you advice. Set a goal and get that meeting on the calendar. Your long-term goal will only be accomplished by setting and achieving smaller goals to get there.
- **Make goals actionable.** For each goal, set targets and create solid concrete plans regarding how to achieve it. If your goal is to improve staff morale in your department, then what are the steps you will take to achieve that goal? What are the action items you can tackle in order to move forward with the goal?
- **Create visibility and accountability.** Keep goals visible. Some people like to print their goals out and post them on a wall where they can be seen. A library will often put their organizational strategic goals and priorities in a report, which is shared with stakeholders in various ways, including on the library's website. At regularly scheduled board meetings, progress toward achieving the goals is discussed. Similarly, an individual can find ways to be held accountable for his or her goals. If you and your supervisor have decided that learning to use the library's makerspace tools is an important and relevant goal for you, then set a time to meet to share your progress.
- **Revisit and revise regularly.** Things change over time. As you work toward a goal, you sometimes realize that assumptions you made in the beginning were inaccurate and you need to make adjustments. Changing a goal is not failure. It is expected and demonstrates that you are staying attuned to needs and reality. For example, if you and your coworker were going to deliver a presentation at the state library conference highlighting your successes with a program, but then your coworker takes a new job in a different state, you will need to revisit your goal to decide whether or not you will continue to achieve. Is there someone else who can work on the presentation with you? Are you willing to deliver the presentation alone? Revise your goal considering the changed situation.
- **Celebrate achievements.** When you reach a goal (and for larger goals, at milestones along the way), celebrate progress and achievements. Completing a large project may warrant a party with balloons

and cake, but even smaller accomplishments deserve recognition. We are often so focused on what we want to be better or different that we forget to appreciate the work that we have done. If you are a supervisor, find ways to recognize the achievements that your team members make with words or recognition of another kind.

- **Learn from your failures.** You are striving to be more disciplined and thoughtful about your time and energy management in order to be more successful. It is inevitable that even the best-laid plans of mice and men often go awry. When things don't go the way you expected, treat that as an opportunity to learn. Talk to others who were involved. Seek to understand and grow. If your goal was to offer a series of financial literacy classes for the community, but no one attended the first program, it doesn't necessarily mean that there's no need for financial literacy skills training in your community. Try to understand the reasons for the failure, revise your goals and plans, and try again.

IDENTIFY PRIORITIES

You may have seen *Multiplicity*, the 1996 Harold Ramis film starring Michael Keaton, in which Keaton's character Doug, feels overwhelmed by his inability to balance his workload and his family life. He tells his wife that they need a schedule and she replies, "We don't need a schedule. We need a miracle!" Doug meets a scientist and is able to clone himself—again and again and again. This solution, however, soon becomes a great big problem. Trying to do way too much never ends well, not for Doug, not for the White Rabbit, not for Hermione. And at least in this century cloning is not the answer. Being realistic about the resources we have available and determining our priorities can help.

When we articulate our priorities, we recognize what is important. We put things in order with the most important thing or things at the top of the list. Getting clear about our priorities ameliorates stress and can help us avoid becoming overwhelmed. By identifying what our priorities are and then developing the habit of focusing on those priorities, we can change our outlooks. Earlier in this chapter, you wrote present goals. Effective time management involves prioritizing those goals and spending time on them, rather than on activities that are not a priority.

There's a strong connection between motivation and priorities. Why do you want to do this? That motivation is what will help you stay committed. I remember hearing a library director explain how clarifying priorities had helped changed the culture of a library. When she was first hired as director, the library had a reputation as a grumpy sort of place. Usage was low and staff morale was, too. Turning the culture around involved not only making it clear that creating a welcoming environment was a top priority, but the director also worked with each staff person individually to learn what mattered to them. Where did their interests and passions lie? This led to shifting duties and roles for a few people and to other changes that helped clarify organizational priorities and align staff member goals and priorities, too. Library usage increased, staff morale dramatically improved, and eventually the library won a national award for exceptional service to its community.

Once you have clearly identified a handful of goals that are going to be priorities for you, then fill out a more detailed worksheet for that specific goal. Consider this worksheet your plan for achieving the goal.

Describe your goal.

Why is this goal a priority?

Start Date:
Target Completion Date:

List the action steps it will take to accomplish this goal.

List the resources needed to accomplish this goal. Include time, money, assistance from others, etc.

List potential obstacles that may impact work toward achieving the goal. For each obstacle, list solutions for handling those obstacles.

How will you know when this goal has been achieved? How will you measure the success of the goal? How will you celebrate the successful achievement of this goal?

CHAPTER 3 KEY TAKEAWAYS

- Analyze time logs and create an activity list that highlights how you have been spending your time.
- Identify things that you want to keep doing and things that you want to change.
- Set five to six goals and write them as SMART goals.
- Effective time management is about prioritizing our goals and spending time on them, rather than on activities that are not a priority.

In this chapter, you have done some of the most important work that you can do when trying to feel like you are effectively managing your time. Identifying goals and priorities is an essential step. Comparing your goals and priorities to the time log you created in the previous chapter is an important way to identify the areas in which time management changes are needed. In the next chapter, you will learn about the basic tools of time management that can be used to help you achieve the goals you have set.

CHAPTER 4

Basic Tools for Time Management

You have determined your goals and priorities, and now it's time to determine how you're going to achieve those things. You are ready to turn your intentions into actions. Like a samurai, you understand your code but now you must choose your weapons. This chapter will cover the weapons of a time management warrior, which are to-do lists, calendars and schedules, clocks and timers, systems, and habits or routines. While the "calendar and clock" is the most important, you must begin with your "to-do list."

TO-DO LISTS

A to-do list is a list of the things we need to accomplish, often prioritized so we can focus on the things that need to be tackled first. As stated earlier, the calendar and clock are the most important; but the to-do list is the most basic time management tool. Technically, it is a *task* management tool. Time and task management are closely related.

You most likely already use to-do lists in your life. Shopping lists, reminders to complete tasks, and checklists for your day are all examples of to-do lists. They may be post-it notes on your refrigerator or pieces of scratch paper at your desk. Some people create a new to-do list each morning, crossing tasks off as they complete them during the day. These short, manageable to-do lists contain items that can be accomplished that day.

Others keep an ongoing task list, adding to it and deleting from it, over days and even weeks. These longer to-do lists have many more tasks than could be completed in a day and may contain the same items from day-to-day.

Researcher Christine Carter, author of *The Sweet Spot*, advocates for also creating a "not to-do" list, too. She emphasizes that we need to be clear not only about what we want to do but also about what we don't want to do. What are the things that distract us from our higher priorities? For example, if you really want to focus on finishing a presentation, then you might include *Checking Facebook* on your "not to-do" list for that day.

Many people find satisfaction in crossing something off their list. As one woman said in reference to her paper to-do list:

> *The satisfaction of being able to manually cross a finished item off the list is a good incentive.*

The sense of accomplishment we feel when we finish something we set out to do becomes an incentive in itself.

There is not one right way to use to-do lists. It is important, however, to be conscious of how your to-do list techniques are helping or hurting you. Also, the items on your to-do list need to be connected to your goals. If they are not, then your goals are not receiving the priority they need in order to be accomplished.

How do you prefer creating and maintaining your to-do list? Do you prefer a simple sticky note on your desk? Do you keep an Excel spreadsheet on your computer, with columns and rows? Do you use an app on your phone? Do you keep a special notebook just to log tasks and related notes? Our individual styles and preferences vary so this section will not prescribe a method for your to-do lists but will instead overview a number of different options for you to explore. Consider the capabilities of the systems you may already use or the new ones discussed next:

- **Google Tasks.** Lots of people who have been using Gmail for years, haven't explored Google Tasks (support.google.com/mail/answer/106237?hl=en), which is available using a mobile app for the Android or iOS mobile operating systems and also via the web. If you are already using Gmail, then it is easy to convert e-mail into tasks. Create tasks with due dates and they will automatically appear on your Google calendar.
- **Microsoft Outlook.** Microsoft Outlook also includes a task list (www.makeuseof.com/tag/use-outlook-simple-task-project-management/), which has reminders and tracking.

- **Evernote.** I have tried a lot of virtual to-do lists, but the one that has "stuck" for me is Evernote (www.evernote.com). It is my favorite app for my smartphone. Use it to create to-do lists and write notes to yourself. You can take photos with your smartphone and include them in a note. You can record voice reminders in Evernote on your smartphone. You can save a web page in a note. Evernote is a powerful tool that allows you to synchronize your notes on virtually any computer, smartphone, or mobile device, and in any web browser. Use the Getting Started guide (www.evernote.com/getting_started) to start exploring this tool.

- **Remember the Milk.** Remember the Milk (www.rememberthemilk .com) is a popular to-do list and a tool to create task reminders for yourself (like a virtual string around your finger). As anyone who uses Remember the Milk will tell you, the simple user interface is one of this tool's strengths. If you're like me, you want the ease of paper to-do lists, but you don't want to keep track of lots of pieces of paper, which is why Remember the Milk is useful. It's almost as easy as a slip of paper, but it won't get lost. As David Allen suggests in *Getting Things Done*, it's important to get things out of your head. I often find myself stressing about something I need to do, worried that I will forget to do it. After I enter it into my electronic to-do list, I feel a sense of relief. Into the tool and out of my mind! There are many nifty things you can do with Remember the Milk, such as e-mailing tasks to a task list and setting up reminder notifications. Use the Getting Started guide (www.rememberthemilk.com/help/guide) to start exploring this handy tool.

- **Toodledo.** Toodledo (www.toodledo.com) is another popular time and task management tool. It is also well suited to the *Getting Things Done* approach, which we will discuss in more depth later in this chapter. In addition to the to-do list functionality, you can use the tool to take notes, make lists, create outlines, and track your habits. You can also collaborate with friends, family, or your coworkers.

- **Bullet Journal.** If, as suggested in earlier chapters, you have started having conversations with people about their preferred time management strategies, it's likely that you will have encountered someone who is a bullet journal user. People who have adopted this method are often passionate about it. It is a print system. You can buy a bullet journal or you can use any notebook. It's a flexible system that includes tasks, events, and notes. Daily logs, monthly logs, and future logs help you create a path to achieving your goals. See http://bulletjournal.com/ to learn more.

- **Passion Planners.** Another analog option that has devoted fans is the passion planner. It helps you break your short- and long-term goals down so you can incorporate them into your daily life. Using it gets you to plan for the future but also to act on it in the present.

The passion planner creates structure for achieving your goals, but there is also room for creativity and reflection. Learn more at http://www.passionplanner.com.

- **Get to Work Books.** Some people have had success using Get to Work Books. These planners include traditional analog planner features such as a year calendar and weekly columns for the seven days of the week. In addition, however, it includes special features like a section in which you "define your own success," weekly columns asking you to identify priority action items, and project breakdown pages at the end of each month, too. See http://www.gettoworkbook.com/ to learn more.

These are tools that have worked well for many people. What works for someone else may be completely different from what works for you. Everyone's brain and everyone's life is unique and there just is not one right solution that will work for everyone.

CALENDARS AND SCHEDULES

Calendars are basic time management tools and the most important of all. Before introducing useful calendar tools, let's take a step back and consider the powerful role calendars play in structuring our lives. Not much is known about timekeeping in prehistoric eras, but artifacts have been discovered that make it clear that in every culture, people were engaged in tracking the passage of time. The school year, for example, has students start their school year in the fall, ending in time for three months of summer vacation. Many activities revolve around this schedule, with families, sports teams, churches, youth groups, and governments basing their activities on the school calendar. Summer reading program is a huge deal for public libraries. Some items in our calendars are imposed by external forces and some items are internally set.

Tracking things in a calendar helps us remember what we need to do and it helps make sure that we don't schedule two things at the same time. Calendars help us structure the time we will need for focus on our priorities. They help us know if we are trying to fit in too many things, assisting us in being mindful about our energy levels, too.

Digital or Print?

Do you use a digital calendar synced between your phone and computer or a print calendar that you carry in your purse or briefcase—or both? Many people keep more than one calendar. You may have a shared online calendar for work, a calendar on the kitchen wall that includes all family activities, or a personal calendar.

Schedules

A schedule is a basic time management technique. To *schedule* means to arrange or plan (an event) to take place at a particular time or to make arrangements to do something. Taking control of your calendar is scheduling. Scheduling involves establishing the things that need to be done and the amount of time doing those things will take and the order in which you will do those things. What needs to be done? How long will it take? In what order should I do things?

There are many examples of library schedules:

- The hours and days the library is open
- Staff schedules—hours that specific employees are expected to be in the library
- Event and programming calendar
- Project management schedules
- Social media calendar

Depending upon your position and responsibilities, these library schedules will help structure your schedule, too. The hours and days the library is open affects your schedule because you are part of the library staffing. The staff schedules will help to make sure that the library is adequately covered during open hours. If you are involved with library events and programming, then those things will shape your schedule, too. If you are working on a project (or projects) with other library team members, then those project schedules will impact your schedule. If you are responsible for the library's social media accounts, then your roles and responsibilities with those accounts may shape your time, too. A social media calendar is a great example of time and task management. Rather than letting posting to the library's social media accounts be something that happens on a whim or when there's a moment of free time, a social media calendar helps you be more intentional about what you are going to post and when.

When focused on time management, we need to consider daily, weekly, monthly, and annual schedules. What do you want to accomplish today? This week? This month? This year? On a daily basis, check in on your tasks and to-do lists. On a weekly or monthly basis, also devote a brief bit of time to reviewing your more long-term goals. Use a simple worksheet like the one from Chapter 3 to track your progress. Note the final section of this worksheet, which is where you can keep notes regarding your progress toward achieving the goal.

Describe your goal.

Why is this goal a priority?

Start Date:
Target Completion Date:

List the action steps it will take to accomplish this goal.

List the resources needed to accomplish this goal. Include time, money, assistance from others, etc.

List potential obstacles that may impact work towards achieving the goal. For each obstacle, list solutions for handling those obstacles.

How will you know when this goal has been achieved? How will you measure the success of the goal? How will you celebrate the successful achievement of this goal?

Month/Day/Year: On a weekly or monthly basis, record your progress toward achieving the goal. Note any accomplishments, any revisions, and any obstacles that you've encountered.

CLOCKS AND TIMERS

It is likely that you have looked at a clock several times today. An alarm clock woke you, a glance at the clock while getting ready let you know how much time you had before you needed to be at work, another glance at the clock led you to roll your eyes at how long your teenager is taking in the shower, and so forth. Once at work, a clock lets you know when to open the library, when to start and end a meeting, when to eat lunch, and when to close the library at the end of the day, too. Time management is seriously impacted by our ability to estimate how long things will take us. Effective use of time involves being able to focus for periods. In this section, we will explore techniques that can help with finding focus, including the Pomodoro Technique, Toomighty, Tomato-Timer, and Timeboxing.

The Pomodoro Technique

Thank goodness for kitchen timers! Without them, how many trays of cookies would have burned? Just knowing that the cookies need to be in the oven for approximately 10 minutes isn't enough. It's easy to get distracted by a phone call and not realize how much time has gone by. We use kitchen timers to help us stay on task. The Pomodoro Technique is based on the tomato-shaped timer that is so common.

The simple technique is based on a belief that our brains work best in 25-minute bursts, followed by a 5-minute break. Every fourth 25-minute burst is followed by a longer break (15 minutes). Why is this simple system effective for so many people? If the time log that you kept revealed that you are easily distracted, this might be a technique for you to try. Sometimes the reason we are easily distracted is because we are bored. We lose our focus on the task at hand because it's more fun to see what new messages might be in our e-mail in-box or what new photos might have been posted on Facebook.

Timer tools help because when you start the timer, you are clearly setting a specific and attainable goal for yourself: focus on this project and on nothing else for 25 minutes. You can then use your 5-minute break for a quick e-mail or Facebook check (although getting up and stretching or walking around for a few minutes might be more rejuvenating and better for your ergonomic well-being).

After trying the Pomodoro technique, one library staff member noted the value of incorporating regular breaks:

I absolutely love the idea of 25 minute energy bursts followed by 5 minute breaks. This is something I really struggle with balancing; I tend to dive head first into a project and work until I can't think straight with it. It's very good to keep the pace of energy and let your mind rest in between (also a good thing to do to lower stress).

You can take this same principle of time management into your workplace by literally bringing a kitchen timer with you to the library. While some people are comfortable with a kitchen timer on their desk, others will be happy to know that technology has created some digital tools that serve the same timer function.

Tomighty

Tomighty (www.tomighty.org) is a timer that you install on your computer. It runs in the system tray. You start the timer and it tracks 25 minutes, dinging to let you know when you should take a break. It then tracks the break (you tell it whether you are taking a short break or a long break). The timer does have flexibility. You can pause the timer if something breaks your 25-minute focus. You can also end your break early and start a new 25-minute section.

TomatoTimer

If you would rather not install an app, there is a web-based tool called TomatoTimer (www.tomato-timer.com). You can access it from anywhere on the web from the device of your choice.

Use of the Pomodoro Technique can help you become aware of time in a different way. It helps us realize how bad we are at estimating time. If I am engrossed in a project, I am shocked that 25 minutes have gone by. If I am struggling to stay focused on something, I find myself watching the Pomodoro, feeling as though time is dragging. Being able to estimate how long a project will take, however, is an important piece of time management. These Pomodoro technique tools can help you improve at your ability to make more accurate estimates. As with the other time management tools and techniques that we have discussed, this is not a one-size-fits-all strategy. Awareness of a timer ticking down in the background makes some people feel very nervous. Another library staff person noted that for her:

> *Pomodoro is great for home, but at work it's rare for me to find 25 uninterrupted minutes.*

SYSTEMS

Timeboxing

Timeboxing is another time management technique that fits with the Pomodoro tools. It's a different way of thinking about time and tasks. With timeboxing, we focus on time instead of tasks. We set an amount of time to work on something. For example, let's say you want to spend more time "keeping up" by reading certain blogs. Timeboxing and setting aside 15 minutes to do this a few times per week would be a good approach. It's about focusing on doing things for the set amount of time (rather than about getting through a certain amount of content). In many library jobs, it's impossible to completely structure our time (we're often responding to and helping others), but there may be certain tasks for which it is a good fit.

Getting Things Done

Time management guru David Allen says, "Your mind is for having ideas, not holding them." Even if you do not completely adopt his Getting Things Done (GTD) system, there are many great ideas in it to consider. The popular productivity system is based on the real-ization that for many people, their calendar manages 3–4 percent of commitments but doesn't track goals, progress, or their to-do list. Instead, we try to keep track of things in our brains and many of us find ourselves going over those mental reminders in the middle of the night. It's that buzz in our brains that causes stress. Allen's answer to this is to create a system that you can trust, in which you capture all of your goals and to-dos. Once you stop trying to keep it all in your head, you have increased capacity to think and be creative. You need room to do what's meaningful without being distracted. It is beyond the scope of this book to completely outline the GTD approach, but a few highlights include:

- **Capture it.** Write everything down. How often have you had a great idea (or even just a useful one) and then you forgot it because you didn't write it down? Keep a paper tray at your desk and use it as an in-box in which you can put notes regarding ideas so you can use them later. Evernote and other tools mentioned earlier in this chapter can be used for a digital version of an in-box, too. If it's time sensitive, then put it in your calendar rather than your in-box.
- **Reflect.** Frequently review what's in your in-box. Don't let things pile up. There's work that must be done to maintain the system. Make time at least weekly to review and make adjustments. It takes time to do, but it helps you feel like you are in control.
- **Review and prioritize.** Daily, either at the end of your day for the following day or right away in the morning, spend time identifying top tasks for the day.
- **The 2-minute rule.** If an item is something that could be completed in two minutes or less, then Allen recommends that you just go ahead and complete it rather than adding it to your system.

Again, these are just a few highlights of the GTD system, but they are useful tips that are fairly easy to implement. If you are interested in diving deeper into GTD, Allen has written a number of books and also maintains the GTD website at www.gettingthingsdone.com.

HABITS AND ROUTINES

Every morning when we wake up and every evening before we go to bed, most of us brush our teeth. It's a habit that we take for granted and barely need to think about. Many of us have taken the advice of our local fire department and when we change the clocks because of daylight savings, we also change and test batteries in our smoke alarms and carbon monoxide detectors. The time changing is not at all related to our smoke alarms, but it's a handy way to make this life-saving task part of our yearly home maintenance routines. Habits and routines are powerful and developing more of them can make a big difference in our time management. We are habit-forming creatures. What can you make routine, so that you don't really even have to think about it?

As anyone who has tried to adopt the habit of regular exercise into their routine can tell you, it takes a while to establish a habit that really sticks. But once it does, things get a whole lot easier. If a morning run becomes part of your routine, then the stress and other negative feelings associated with not exercising go away. You've just done it! Think about the habits and routines that are in place at the library where you work. Do you have opening and closing procedures that you follow? Often we have systems in place and we develop habits to use those systems.

Diana Weaver, director of a small library in northeast Kansas, talks about the value routines play in her work:

> We created an Annual Board Calendar of Events that lists per month events that reoccur each year; for instance tax distributions, staff in-service, annual meetings, etc. The calendar also includes one designated policy per month from our policy manual. The goal is that the board will review every policy at least once every three years. Of course, that's flexible depending on immediate need for discussion of a particular policy. The Board Calendar of Events helps me when I write my director's report and helps set each month's board meeting agenda.

Think about the habits you currently have at work, especially related to your time usage. What do you do when you first arrive at work? What do you do before your break, after a break, or at the end of the day? Are there bad habits that are holding you back? How can you develop new habits and routines that will help you move forward in achieving your goals? It takes willpower, but the effect can be powerful.

CHAPTER 4 KEY TAKEAWAYS

- To-do lists, calendars and schedules, clocks and timers, systems, and habits or routines are the weapons available to time management warriors.
- To-do lists help us set our intention to work toward our goals. There is not one right way to create or use to-do lists. Numerous print and digital options exist.
- Scheduling helps you take control of your calendar. Be sure you are scheduling time to work on your goals.
- Using a timer can help you find periods of time to focus on a task.
- Timeboxing is a way to be deliberate about working on something for a set amount of time.
- Getting Things Done is a productivity plan that advocates getting things out of your head and into a system.
- Developing habits and routines can make a powerful difference in making progress toward your goals.

In this chapter, we have explored some of the most basic tools of successful time management. In the next several chapters, we will review some of the most common obstacles to time management.

CHAPTER 5

Getting Past Procrastination

Even with the perfect to-do list, an organized calendar, and the intention to achieve, we sometimes don't accomplish as much as we would like. Changes, interruptions, and unexpected developments can lead to delays, but sometimes it is not external factors getting in our way. It is our own procrastination that is keeping us from doing what needs to be done. This chapter defines procrastination and suggests ways to combat a person's procrastinating.

WHAT IS PROCRASTINATION?

To procrastinate is to intentionally put off doing something that should be done. It's a familiar scenario. Debbie has a project that she needs to complete, but rather than focusing on it, she has been browsing social media and socializing with her colleagues. She is procrastinating and putting off taking action on a task that needs to be completed.

When we procrastinate, we voluntarily put off actions, even though we know that we should be working on them. Often when we procrastinate, we're focused on short-term gratification rather than on longer-term achievement and goal accomplishment.

It can be tricky to identify procrastination when we are doing it. Sometimes we may be conducting a valid and useful activity, but if it is at the expense of an activity that should be our current priority and focus, then it is procrastination. If I should be working on a report for the library board, but instead I decide to organize the storage closet, I'm not wasting time, but I'm putting off what really needs to be done. If I have an expense report that I should be completing but jump at the opportunity to help a colleague do something he could easily do himself, then I'm procrastinating.

Procrastination is not always a bad thing. There are times when putting off making a decision or taking action is the best choice. If you are being asked to make a decision about something and don't feel you have enough information or that you have had enough time to really think it over, procrastination can help us not make hasty errors in judgement. For example, if a library director is thinking about pursuing virtual reality technology, but is not sure where or how it's a good fit in the library, then putting off that decision is not a bad thing. It's clear that more research and exploration and maybe just more time are needed.

WHY DO WE PROCRASTINATE?

A bit of procrastination is normal and natural. If it is sabotaging us, however, then it becomes a problem. Some reasons that we may procrastinate include:

- You find the task boring. For example, you really should finish that paperwork, but you're finding it hard to stay motivated because browsing book lists is more fun.
- You are not confident that you have the skills or knowledge necessary to successfully accomplish the task. When you're not sure how to tackle a task, it sometimes feels easier to avoid it.
- You feel overwhelmed by a large project. When getting started with a big project, it can be really hard to know where to begin, so sometimes you put off the start.
- You are overextended and have underestimated how much time your tasks will take. Have you said "yes" one too many times and now your to-do list is longer than one person can reasonably handle?
- You are afraid of failure and protect yourself with the excuse that you ran out of time. When working on a challenging project, the final stages can be the most stressful. High school guidance counselors talk about the epidemic of seniors who drop out with only a credit or two to complete. Fear of failure is real and it can keep people from completing important things.
- You resent feeling controlled by the person who assigned the task. Maybe your boss gave you critical feedback about a project and now you are struggling to feel motivated to complete it.
- You lack time and task management skills and need more discipline. When we're surrounded by other people (or have a connection to the Internet) there is always something fun and engaging that can occupy our time—sometimes at the expense of the things that really need to be accomplished.

- You are distracted by other problems or situations, either personal or at work. When you are dealing with a difficult situation, it can be extremely difficult to find the focus and motivation needed to complete tasks.
- Your work environment is distracting and is not conducive to focusing on a project. If people are always stopping by your desk to chat or if they are even just having conversations nearby, it can be hard to focus. I once had a job with a lot of fabulous and friendly coworkers. While I loved talking to them, I also found myself needing to stay late to complete work after others had gone home for the night.
- Depression, ADHD, or other conditions are keeping you from being able to focus and complete tasks.

As you can see, procrastination is not always a problem of time management. The reasons are sometimes more complex.

ADDRESSING PROCRASTINATION

Just as effective time management can be learned, we can also learn to address our procrastination. Keeping a time log and being reflective about our time management challenges can provide insights into our behavior. If you think that procrastination is a problem for you, there are strategies you can try to tackle the aforementioned general challenges.

- **Pay attention to your patterns.** Are there certain types of tasks that you regularly procrastinate doing? Do you procrastinate when something is boring? Or when you feel overwhelmed?
- **Break large projects down into smaller tasks.** It's natural to feel overwhelmed when facing a huge task. Breaking it down into more manageable parts can help.
- **Give yourself deadlines.** Some people need the pressure of deadlines in order to move forward with a project. Schedule an appointment to discuss a project with your boss so you have the pressure of needed to be prepared for that meeting.
- **Just get started.** Sometimes getting started is the hardest part. If you feel tempted to procrastinate, push yourself to spend just 10 minutes on a project, rather than putting it off. Often, once you get started, you will probably keep going.
- **Reward yourself for progress.** Give yourself a treat for accomplishing a task. Tell yourself that you can only take a coffee break, eat an ice-cream cone, or leave work early if you complete a task that needs to be done.
- **We are often impacted by the procrastination of others.** One way to address this is to make individual contributions and responsibilities and accountability clear to all. Openly communicate who is responsible for what and when it needs to be accomplished.

If you're feeling this . . .	Then try this . . .
"This is really boring."	• Reward yourself when you complete a mundane task. • Make dull tasks more engaging by listening to music as you complete them. • "Gamify" the task in some way –by giving yourself time challenges, for example.
"I'm really struggling to focus on this when I'm so worried about something else . . ."	• If you are experiencing a major life problem, then you may need to be realistic with yourself and with others about what you will be able to accomplish. If you are dealing with a temporary life situation (such as a sick family member), you need to understand that your work output and abilities may be less than they normally are and adapt accordingly. • If possible, address the problem that is consuming your attention.
"I've got too much to do. I can't get it all done."	• Make a list of the projects and tasks you need to complete. Sort them by priority level and due date. Work on the highest priority item that is due first. • Just get started. What can you accomplish today? • Delegate to others. Are any of the projects or tasks things that you can delegate to others? • Take unnecessary tasks off your plate. Are there things on your to-do list that you don't really need to do? Cross them off and focus on the things that matter.

Am I a Procrastinator?

Use this worksheet to identify your own procrastination tendencies, applying what you have learned to your experience. Identify your challenges and then create action steps for tacking this time management obstacle.

Questions

- Do you frequently find yourself turning in projects late or hurrying to complete tasks at the last minute?
- Are you guilty of putting things off until tomorrow, or next week, or next month?
- Does it take the pressure of an approaching deadline to motivate you to complete a project or task?

Reflection Take a few minutes to think about the role this potential time management issue plays in your life. Write your thoughts here. Questions to consider include: is this a time management issue for me? Are there positive elements of being a procrastinator? When is this the biggest challenge for me?

Strategies to Try

- Get to the root of *why* you procrastinate. Is it fear of failure? Boredom? Lack of adequate time?
- Big projects can be overwhelming. Focus on taking small steps and completing manageable tasks.
- Be realistic about the amount of time you have, the amount of time tasks will take, and the necessary quality of your work.

My Action Steps What actions will you take to try to conquer this time management issue? List your ideas here. Remember that change takes time so give new strategies a chance.

Stephanie Gerding is a librarian and grant-writing expert. If you have ever written a grant application, then you know that it can be a daunting task (and very tempting to procrastinate). Two of Gerding's favorite pieces of advice for would-be grant writers are "Baby steps are OK" and "Deadlines are not optional." Both are really great time management tips! Gerding stresses the importance of these two simple rules:

> *A big grant proposal and project can be intimidating. If you're already busy, how are you going to find the time to write a grant proposal and then implement the project if you get it? By taking baby steps and giving yourself deadlines! Time seems to slip away without deadlines set to remind you to focus on your goals. Working on project for even an hour or two per week can really add up over time. You'll make progress. You'll make things happen.*

It is an advice that is useful not only for would-be grant writers but for all of us as we consider how to manage our tendency to procrastinate.

CHAPTER 5 KEY TAKEAWAYS

- Procrastination keeps us from working on what needs to be done.
- Some procrastination is normal and natural and can even be beneficial.
- There are many reasons people procrastinate. Some reasons are external and others are internal.
- It is possible to learn to overcome procrastination. Understanding the reason you are procrastinating is key, then appropriate actions can be taken.

In this chapter, we have reviewed the ways in which procrastination impacts time management. There are many reasons people procrastinate, but there are also ways to address and move past the obstacles it creates. In the next chapter, we'll tackle another common time management challenge: perfectionism.

CHAPTER 6

Overcoming Perfectionism:
Yours and Others

Many people deny perfectionist tendencies. The perfectionist deems anything less than perfection as unacceptable. They often feel like what they do and how they do it is so far from perfect that it is not fitting to describe their style as perfectionistic. Some of you may see the topic for this chapter and decide you aren't a perfectionist and maybe you don't need to read the chapter. However, even if it does not feel like it is an issue that is currently relevant for you and you do not feel you exhibit perfectionist tendencies, almost every organization has perfectionist individuals on staff. That alone makes this an important topic and one that is often neglected when discussing time management. This chapter explains perfectionism and how to deal with it in yourself and others.

WATCHING PERFECTIONISM

Books, TV shows, and movies are filled with characters who are perfectionists. Hermione Granger in the *Harry Potter* series represents this archetype. She regards anything short of perfection as unacceptable. At its best, perfectionism is associated with high standards and a desire for achievement. At its worst, perfectionism can cause depression, anxiety, stress, and low self-esteem. There is a difference between the desire to excel and the desire to be perfect. In her book *Gifts of Imperfection*, Brené Brown states:

> *Understanding the difference between healthy striving and perfectionism is critical to laying down the shield and picking up your life. Research shows that perfectionism hampers success. In fact, it's often the path to depression, anxiety, addiction, and life paralysis.*

There are different types of perfectionists. Some perfectionists have unrealistic standards for themselves and focus on their own flaws. Other perfectionists have unrealistic expectations of the people around them. Yet another type of perfectionist believes that other people expect him or her to be perfect.

Several things may be associated with perfectionism:

- Excessive worry over making mistakes
- Extremely high personal standards
- Self-doubt about the quality of one's actions

Perfectionism can have a powerful impact on time management and on job performance. Here are a few of the ways in which perfectionism shows up in the workplace.

- **Burnout.** Perfectionism drains your energy and it can lead to burnout.
- **Procrastination.** Perfectionism is often behind procrastination in the workplace. An employee can become so overwhelmed by the desire to complete a task or project perfectly that he or she cannot even get started on the project.
- **Inability to start.** During brainstorming or planning, a perfectionistic employee may become overly focused on creating a perfect plan, to the point that the actual project itself never gets started.
- **Stress.** Perfectionism can lead to stress. If you constantly feel the pressure to complete each project to an unrealistic level of perfection, then you will probably feel quite stressed.
- **Overemphasis on control.** Time management tools can become harmful in the hands of a perfectionist. Focusing too much on details, lists, rules, order, organization, and schedules, can lead you to lose sight of the major point of what you are trying to accomplish.
- **Failure to complete tasks.** A rigid adherence to perfectionist standards often interferes with the ability to complete tasks. So, if you have a coworker who cannot get work done on time or cannot meet deadlines, it's possible that his or her perfectionism prevents him or her from completing tasks because they feel their work must be perfect.
- **Unwilling to take risks.** If you are afraid of making mistakes, you will probably not be willing to take risks. Perfectionism gets in the way of innovation.

- **Difficulty collaborating.** Perfectionists are not always good at collaborating with others, especially if they set the same unrealistic standards for others that they set for themselves.

DEALING WITH PERFECTIONISM

Are you a perfectionist? Do you rarely feel satisfied with the work you have done? Do you often feel like the things you've done could have been done better? Do you frequently also lay awake at night rehearsing how you could have improved a conversation that you had at work? If the answer is "yes," it's likely that you have perfectionist tendencies. Take heart, however. There are techniques and words of advice that can help you address and move beyond this inclination.

1. **You don't need to get an A+ on everything.** When my friend's daughter was in high school, she was not satisfied with receiving *A* grades. Instead, she expected herself to get perfect scores on everything. This sort of perfectionist behavior can carry over into the workplace and we can find ourselves trying to do everything at a level that "exceeds expectations." I'm not saying you shouldn't care about the quality of your work. However, there are certain tasks for which it is fine to simply finish the task, rather than finish it in an exceptional way.
2. **Strive to be efficient, not perfect.** Deadlines can move us along. There's no room for perfectionism if we're focused on getting something done as quickly and efficiently as possible. Sometimes it's OK to focus on getting something done, rather than on getting it done exceptionally.
3. **Focus on the things that matter.** If we are trying to do *everything* extremely well, then we're most likely spreading our energies around among too many things. Return to the list of priorities you created in Chapter 3. Focus your energies on those priorities and let other things go as much as you can.
4. **Take a step back.** Perfectionists tend to get bogged down in details. If you think you may be doing that with a project, force yourself to take a step back and look at things from a broader perspective. Which details really matter? If things don't happen just as you plan, what's the worst that could happen? What will matter a month from now?
5. **Ask for help.** Rather than feeling that you need to do things entirely on your own, realize that there are others who can help you. Ask for advice. Talk over challenges. Request help when needed.

Even if you are not a perfectionist, you probably know someone who is. If someone who works for you is a perfectionist and is being held back by their perfectionism, you can help. In addition to encouraging them to try to be OK with less than perfect results on every single task, experiment with other strategies, too. Here are a few ideas:

- One suggestion is to give them so much to do that they don't have time to obsess over any one thing. Alternately ask them to work on only one project for a time.
- When assigning tasks, have a conversation about expectations regarding quality and time to be spent.
- It is important that a supervisor be able to give feedback, yet giving constructive feedback to a perfectionist can be challenging. Help the perfectionist see that feedback is about a project or task and is not about their worth as a person or employee.
- An openness to risk and willingness to experiment are essential skills and mind-sets for creativity and innovation. Help the perfectionist realize that some failure is to be expected from a creative individual can aid his or her shift away from detrimental perfectionist traits.

Helping a perfectionist understand and handle his or her tendencies can be a delicate matter, but with tact and positive framing, you may be able to provide the guidance and support the individual needs in gaining a more realistic perspective. At the end of the day, most of us, perfectionists, almost perfectionists, or non-perfectionists learn that there is value in making mistakes. That's often where learning begins.

THE VALUE OF MAKING MISTAKES

As we work to develop time management skills, it is important to remember that efficiency is not always the ultimate marker of success. Organizations that are focused on learning and innovation need to sometimes approach things in a way that is not linear and planned. Ultimately it is beneficial to create a work culture in which everyone understands that mistakes are expected. If you encourage innovation and risk taking, then mistakes are inevitable. Worry about imperfect results not only holds individuals back, but it also holds organizations back. Mistakes are a necessary aspect of the creative process. By-products of the creative process can become new ideas and initiatives. Pilot projects, beta tests, and experiments are all ways to try something out. They are a way to learn.

How can we create workplace cultures in which it really is OK to make mistakes? Sometimes it takes modeling by leaders. Elaine Wherry, one of the founders of the chat site Meebo, recorded the mistakes she made as an employee and manager. She recorded them in sketchbooks, using notes and drawings. She shared this with her employees. In some cases, this may have helped them avoid making the same mistakes, but it also just made it clear that mistakes were likely to happen, which helped the employees see it as a normal part of the process. In addition to modeling that it's OK to make mistakes,

Am I a Perfectionist?

Use this worksheet to identify your own perfectionist tendencies, applying what you have learned to your experience. Identify your challenges and then create action steps for tackling this time management obstacle.

Questions
- Do you rarely feel satisfied with your work on tasks or projects?
- Do you obsess over mistakes you make or criticism you receive?
- Do you recognize your strengths and weaknesses? Or do you feel the need to be good at everything?

Reflection Take a few minutes to think about the role this potential time management issue plays in your life. Write your thoughts here. Questions to consider include: is this a time management issue for me? Are there positive elements of being a perfectionist? When is this the biggest challenge for me?

Strategies to Try
- Recognize that sometimes good enough really is good enough. Learn to prioritize which things are high priority and worth extra time and energy.
- Accept that you are human and will make mistakes (and accept this about others, too). See mistakes as learning opportunities.
- Keep the aphorism "Perfect is the enemy of good" in mind and recognize that perfectionism can keep us from getting a lot of good work done.

My Action Steps What actions will you take to try to conquer this time management issue? List your ideas here. Remember that change takes time so give new strategies a chance.

it's also useful to build in processes and systems that support reflection and learning. For example, after a failure or mistake, taking the time to openly discuss what happened and what can be learned from it is incredibly powerful, but rarely done. There's a tendency to avoid openly and constructively talking about what did not go well. However, it's only by doing so that we can learn and improve, personally and organizationally. http://blogs.wsj.com/atwork/2013/03/29/the-manager-who-kept-a-six-year-diary-of-her-mistakes.

CHAPTER 6 KEY TAKEAWAYS

- There is a difference between striving for excellence and perfectionism.
- Perfectionism can have a negative impact on time management.
- The burnout, stress, inefficiency, and inability to complete projects and tasks are all potential effects of perfectionism.
- Asking for assistance is a step to take to get past perfectionism.
- The understanding that mistakes are not only OK, but expected may result in greater organizational innovation.

In this chapter, we have reviewed the ways in which perfectionism impacts time management. Perfectionism is a more common challenge than we may realize, but there are ways to address and move past the obstacles it creates. In the next chapter, we'll tackle another common time management challenge: interruptions and distractions.

CHAPTER 7

Dealing with Distractions and Interruptions

While there are different causes for distractions and interruptions, the outcome is often similar—inability to focus on goals and priorities. A distraction or an interruption draws your attention away from what you are supposed to be paying attention to. For example, if you are trying to work on a project, but shift your attention to your e-mail every time you hear a "ding" letting you know that you have a new message, then e-mail is serving as a distraction. When your colleague stops by your desk to tell you about his favorite sport's team's win, that can be an interruption.

You start your day with a list of tasks, determined to check them all off before you leave ay 5:00 PM. As the day goes on, however, you are pulled in different directions and situations arise that need your immediate attention, more than the items on your task list. In my experience, dealing with interruptions is the greatest time management challenge cited by people working in libraries.

DEFINING DISTRACTIONS AND INTERRUPTIONS

Daydreaming, social media, and workplace activity can all be potential distractions. Likewise, an interruption is also something that draws your attention away from what you are supposed to be paying attention to, for example, as stated earlier, someone coming by your desk to ask you to talk to you, or a phone call. Everyone deals with distractions and interruptions in the workplace to some extent. Potential distractions include:

- Environmental (You are too hot or too cold)
- Technological (Your library Wi-Fi is down)
- Coworkers (Conversations happening near your desk)
- Phone alerts (You have a new message or notification)
- Social media (Constantly checking what's happening)
- E-mail (New messages that draw your attention)
- Loud noises (Construction work nearby)

In *Driven to Distraction at Work: How to Focus and Be More Productive*, author Ned Hallowell, adds six common distractions in the workplace to the aforementioned list including: feeling addicted to our devices, trying to focus on multiple things at once, jumping from project to project, worrying about things rather than working on them, fixing everyone else's problems, and "dropping the ball" (not getting organized and underachieving at work). Using the following sheet, list your distractions and interruptions in the 14 areas and then decide which are necessary and which are unnecessary.

It is important to note that not all distractions or interruptions are bad! You need to differentiate between necessary interruptions and unnecessary interruptions. Knowing our priorities can help you do that. When keeping a time log, one children's librarian discovered her distractions were sometimes relevant to her job.

> *I use Pinterest a lot to look for activities to do, flyer ideas, display ideas, book lists etc. and I find that I get side tracked by new ideas when I see something on there. Usually it's just a few seconds of clicking the "pin it" button but other times I'll go read the article or look at the website and then I am off on a new tangent. I'm starting to think of it as the "oh, shiny!" effect. I'm not sure if this is always a bad thing though as most of these ideas are useful and are relevant to my work.*

Other examples of necessary and positive distractions include:

- Time spent building community and connecting via the library's social media accounts
- Time spent talking to other staff about immediate library challenges
- Time spent building relationships with coworkers
- Time spent providing assistance to library users
- Time spent browsing websites relevant to a program you are planning

One library manager reviewed her time log and noticed how much time she spent talking to staff.

Use this worksheet to identify the distractions and interruptions that impact you. For each type, describe the examples that you specifically experience. Check either necessary or unnecessary as appropriate. For each distraction or interruption that you have marked unnecessary, suggest solutions for fixing the problem.

Distraction or Interruption type:	Your examples of this type of distraction	Necessary	Unnec cessary	How to fix the unnecessary
Environmental				
Technological				
Coworkers				
Library users				
Phone alerts				
Social media				
E-mail				
Loud noises				
Addicted to devices				
Too many things to do at one time				
Jumping from project to project				
Worrying about things rather than fixing them				
Fixing everyone else's Problems				
Dropping the ball				

I was surprised by how many hours I logged as "staff con-versations." By this, I mean mostly unplanned exchanges with clerks and librarians about how their work is going and what they need. I felt good about discovering the amount of time spent on these conversations. Maybe if I consciously dedicated a chunk of time to this activity each day, I would cut down on the number of interruptions by staff when I need to be working on other projects because they already would have had a chance to pose their questions and get answers.

Distractions and interruptions are a factor in any workplace. Now that you have identified them in your workplace, you're ready to start addressing the things that can be changed.

THE VALUE OF FOCUS

Despite misconceived public notions of library work as peaceful book centered solitude, library work environments are often not conducive to long periods of uninterrupted focus. Whether it is coworkers needing to collaborate or library users needing assistance, the library workplace is a busy environment. The variety of tasks and the many opportunities to make a difference are what attracted many of us to the field. Yet, the ability to focus on tasks is a powerful time management tool. How can you find a balance between staying engaged with the present moment needs in your workplace while also focusing on tasks and projects that need undivided attention? Ask yourself these questions about your own work style and work environment:

- Are you able to concentrate on a project or task for at least ½ hour at a time without being interrupted by a library user, coworker, or your phone?
- Do you sometimes keep your attention on a task for at least ½ hour at a time without being drawn to a distraction such as e-mail?
- Is your workspace conducive to focused time?
- Is there an alternative space you can use when you need to spend focused time?

Finding this space might mean working at home or in a conference room. Is that allowed and even encouraged in your organization?

List the alternate places in your library where you or others could work without distraction.

If you are working with focus, then you have a clear direction, you follow through, and you are able to stay on track. When you are able to focus on one thing for an extended period of time, it is amazing how high your quality of work is and how quickly you can get it done. Even brief times during which you are able to focus can help you feel happier and less stressed. Although some people seem better able to tune out distractions than others, people are not born with the power of focus. It is a skill that needs to be developed. Administrators can also help by recognizing the need for focused work time and can support workplace spaces and practices that foster it.

While times of focus are important, it's also good to note that taking regular breaks from mental tasks improves your productivity and creativity. As stated in Chapter 2, our brains work best in 25-minute bursts, followed by a 5-minute break. Every fourth 25-minute burst is followed by a longer break (15 minutes). This helps keep our focus on the task at hand because we have five minutes to check new messages that might be in our e-mail in-box.

Skipping breaks can lead to exhaustion and stress. Does taking a break make you feel guilty? Don't! You need to regularly disconnect from a project or task to recharge internally. Things you could do include:

- Go for a walk
- Read a book
- Do a crossword puzzle
- Write
- Color
  - Draw

When you return to your work, you may find your ability to focus has returned.

DEALING WITH DISTRACTIONS AND INTERRUPTIONS

You know the feeling, you've got a full plate of tasks to complete and then someone calls your name, needing you to tackle another issue. The conflicting desires, to help and to accomplish our goals, can create a sense of pressure or stress. By anticipating the pressure, you can plan for it and feel less stress.

- **The first step is awareness.** Be aware of the interrupters in your workflow. When logging time, keep track not only of what you do but also track when you are interrupted.
- **Plan for distractions.** Effective time management involves realistically setting goals that we can accomplish within the time we have available. If you're frequently interrupted, then overestimate how long tasks are going to take.
- **Limit distractions.** Some distractions cannot be avoided and need to be prioritized (responding to a crisis or an opportunity). There are some distractions, however, that can be avoided. E-mail is one. Social media is another. While working on a project, take a break from checking them. Don't have audible notifications on.
- **Communicate "unavailable" and "available" time.** For example, a director who needs to work on the budget and cannot be interrupted for minor things can find a way to let her staff know. Use this technique judiciously. If part of your job is to be available to help people or if you're a manager and need to be available during a crisis, then you don't want to be completely unavailable too often.
- **Set parameters for interruptions.** If you are interrupted while working on an important task, be clear about your availability. You could say, "I have a couple of minutes right now or we could meet tomorrow." Be firm yet friendly. Susan is a librarian who shared that her challenge was actually her boss, who kept stopping by her desk to talk at length about various issues and topics. Susan bravely had

a conversation with her boss about her time management goals and asked her boss if it would be possible to schedule a one hour weekly meeting. Now when her boss stops by her desk and starts to talk at length, Susan is sometimes able to say, "That seems like a really important issue and I'll make a note so we remember to discuss it at our meeting on Friday."

- **Find a workspace that is conducive to focused attention.** If it's an option, relocate to a conference room or another quiet space to complete a task that requires focus and attention.

- **Be aware of workplace activity trends.** By logging your time usage, you become aware of your own energy patterns (tired after lunch, most alert around 10:00 AM). It's also useful to be aware of activity level trends in the workplace. Is it normally quiet on Wednesday mornings? Always busy at 3:00 PM? Consider these trends as you plan your day.

- **Consider purchasing noise cancelling headphones.** One library technician said, "When I really need to focus on a task, then I use my headphones to shut out all the noise."

- **Remember that energy levels matter.** In addition to environmental factors, physiological factors need to be addressed, too. Is where you are working too cold, too hot? Are you well rested? Have you eaten lunch? These things will impact your ability to really concentrate.

Are Distractions and Interruptions a Time Management Issue for Me?

Use this worksheet to identify the distractions and interruptions that impact your time management, applying what you have learned in this chapter to your experience. Identify your challenges and then create action steps for tackling this time management obstacle.

Questions
- Are you able to find ½ hour blocks of uninterrupted time to focus on a project or task when needed?
- Can you spend ½ hour concentrating on a project or task or do you find yourself distracted (by email or Facebook, for example)?
- Does your workplace layout make it difficult to focus on a project or task without interruptions?

Reflection Take a few minutes to think about the role this potential time management issue plays in your life. Write your thoughts here. Questions to consider include: is this a time management issue for me? Are there positive elements of distractions and interruptions? When is this the biggest challenge for me?

Strategies to Try
- If distractions are a challenge, set concentration time goals for yourself. Set a timer for ½ hour and set the intention of staying focused on a project or task for that block of time.
- Find ways to gracefully let others know that you need time and space to focus on a project or task. This may include putting a sign on a door, scheduling conversations (rather than having them on the fly), and moving to quiet or secluded areas when concentrated focus time is needed.
- If it is not possible to regularly find extended blocks of interrupted time in your work day, then learn to break your tasks down into small pieces that can be accomplished in shorter time spans.

My Action Steps What actions will you take to try to conquer this time management issue? List your ideas here. Remember that change takes time so give new strategies a chance.

CHAPTER 7 KEY TAKEAWAYS

- Distractions and interruptions are a significant time management challenge in many library workplaces.
- Some distractions are internally imposed (shifting attention to Facebook) and some are externally imposed (coworker conversations).
- Not all distractions and interruptions are bad.
- Focus is important for effective completion of tasks. However, taking regular breaks is important, too.
- Strategies, from direct communication to noise cancelling headphones, can help create a workplace environment that supports uninterrupted time when it is needed.

In this chapter, we have discussed one of the time management challenges that is most prevalent for those working in libraries: distractions and interruptions. While distractions and interruptions are inevitable, there are times in which focus is needed in order to complete tasks and projects. The strategies discussed make it clear that time management is not something that happens in isolation but instead is something that must be created within the context of our work environments. In the next chapter, we'll expand our analysis of the impact of others on our time management, by looking at ways in which time management is impacted by collaboration.

CHAPTER 8

Collaboration

The way all of us learn and work is becoming increasingly collaborative. Even if you, as an individual, are an incredibly effective time manager, it is likely that you do not work in a self-contained environment. Your ability to manage time effectively is impacted by working as part of a team. Although it is beyond the scope of this book to cover project management, collaborative time management is a significant topic that must be addressed. Time management books and articles frequently ignore collaboration and its impact on time management. Due to the increasingly collaborative nature of the ways in which library staff work, however, it's a topic that cannot be ignored. The chapter starts with the value of collaboration and the nature of collaboration. It also gives you some tools to use to improve the effectiveness and efficiency with which you collaboratively work to manage time.

THE VALUE OF COLLABORATION

As you start this chapter on collaboration and time management, it's important to recognize the benefits collaboration provides. Collaboration means to work together, usually for the benefit of both parties or for the benefit of a project or organization. Cooperation and teamwork are important in almost any environment, but collaboration goes beyond those two things. Collaboration is about actually creating something together. For the most part everyone agrees that collaboration is a good thing, but many have not clarified the value it brings to their library or exactly why to collaborate.

- At its best, collaboration can help an organization save money, time, and energy. By working together toward a goal, synergy and shared knowledge can strengthen processes and products. If related communication and processes are not mindfully addressed, however, collaboration can create extra work and frustration for the parties involved. It takes work to effectively collaborate. Goals, priorities, and deadlines (time management tools you have read about in this book) all need to be articulated and adhered to for collaboration to work well.
- Ultimately, a collaboration will draw upon the strengths of the parties that are involved and will lead to better quality outputs than any of the parties could achieve on their own. If an art center and a library collaborate on an art and literature program for youth, then the library can benefit from the skills and knowledge the art center brings to the table. The art center will benefit from the literary knowledge that the library staff bring to the table. In the end, the collaboration will lead to a stronger program than either organization could have achieved on its own.
- Collaboration can lead to innovation. The synergy that can be found in mutually beneficial relationships can lead to interesting new developments. For example, an academic library that collaborates with the history department to create a display and program as part of a community 100th anniversary celebration will ultimately have a richer and more unique output than either entity could have created on its own.

While there are many benefits, it's important to recognize that collaboration is not always appropriate. Sometimes, a task or project can be accomplished more efficiently and just as effectively as a solo effort. It is frustrating when simple tasks are made overly complicated and people end up in meetings and discussions, struggling to reach consensus on something that does not warrant the effort. Remember that teamwork and collaboration are not the same thing. You work together as part of a team, each fulfilling your responsibilities and relying on one another in order to get jobs done. To collaborate, you are actually working together to create something. I once heard someone suggest that *cocreators* was a good synonym to use for collaborators, and I think it helps clarify the meaning.

THE NATURE OF COLLABORATION

Collaboration can be between two people or it can be among a much larger group. When you need to collaborate on a project, do you think, "Great! The end result will be better because we're working together." Or do you find yourself thinking, "Ugh, working on it as a group is going to be slow and will involve a lot of pointless meetings. I wish I could just do it myself." If you are like most people, sometimes you think the former and sometimes you feel the latter. Your perspective changes based upon the nature of the tasks and the individuals who compose the team. When you are working on more routine activities, collaboration is often not the answer, but when you want to do something innovative or when you want to identify new solutions to a problem, then collaboration can be the best answer.

Leading Collaboration

Collaboration can increase or decrease the productivity of individuals in the team. Individual participation and accountability, leadership, and coordination can increase the quality of the group's output and decrease the stress level of everyone involved. How can you effectively lead collaborative efforts?

- Clarify goals and purpose. What is the point of the collaboration? Is there a problem that needs to be solved? Is there an opportunity to work together to address needs in the community? Each involved party should be aware of the goals and intentions of the others in the collaboration. Some will be shared, but some will be unique. For example, a library that is collaborating with a local business to provide a community event will need to understand that one of the business's goals is to gain positive publicity for the endeavor. Being clear about expectations from the start will help make the relationship most positive.
- Specify roles and responsibilities. Who will do what? The best collaborations draw upon the strengths of those involved, with little duplication of efforts. The leader of the collaborative effort should be working to identify the strengths of the various members in order to share the workload appropriately.
- Communicate regularly and effectively. As the leader of a collaborative effort, share progress updates on a regular basis.

Virtual Collaboration

An increased amount of work and collaboration is done virtually. This creates new opportunities, but it also creates some challenges. How do you keep a project on track when the various individuals who are working on it are all around the region, the country or even around the world? Some of the relationship building that naturally happens when individuals are meeting face-to-face regularly will need to be emphasized more overtly in a virtual collaboration.

Whether work is being done with people in the same physical building or with people who are located in different locations, the elements required for successful *individual* time management are also key factors for effective time management in collaborative efforts. Shared calendars, to-do lists, and other time management tools help. In addition, systems for tracking resources and ideas are useful, too. Successful collaborations require:

- **Shared goals and priorities.** The individuals who are collaborating need to be on the same page with clear objectives and agreed-upon goals.
- **Shared understandings of task ownership.** You have to be able to count on the work of others and you need to be accountable for the work that others expect from you.
- **Shared timelines and deadlines.** Earlier in the book we discussed the importance of calendars, schedules, and deadlines. If you are working on a project alone, this is important. If you are working with others, it is imperative. Individuals need to be aware not only of their own deadlines but also the deadlines that others are working toward. It is quite likely that the timeline you first establish will need to be modified along the way. This is not a sign of failure. It's important to have a plan and communicate when you encounter unexpected events and unavoidable delays.
- **Open communication about expectations and shared work.** Elsewhere in this book, you have been encouraged to have conversations with others about time management. It's important to talk about time management approaches, challenges, and expectations with those with whom you collaborate.
- **Accountability.** If others are not effectively managing their time and it is impacting you or others in the group, then being able to refer to previous conversations about timelines, deadlines, and workload can help alleviate the problems.
- **Good documentation.** In your personal time management, you may use to-do lists, tools for keeping notes, and goal lists with action items. These sorts of documents need to be kept for group work, too. Rather than depending on e-mails, shared folders are handy and easier to update and keep organized. Include a systematic approach to tracking relevant resources and ideas.

TOOLS FOR COLLABORATION

As seen in previous chapters, technology can help more effectively manage time and tasks. While it is relatively easy for you to try a variety of technological tools as an individual, it is more difficult to initiate usage of a tool by a group. If you are not the leader of the group, you may not have the ability to suggest that a particular tool be used. You can explore the tools in this section as an individual, so that you can get a feel for their usefulness before suggesting that a group use them. Some tools do not require adoption by a work team but can just be used "on the fly" by responding to a link or web-based form.

Doodle (www.doodle.com)

It is a free, simple, no frills tool, but Doodle makes scheduling meetings with a group much easier. If you're trying to decide on a meeting time, you can set up a Doodle poll with the various dates and times that are possibilities. Meeting invitees then indicate the dates and times that would work for them. You can then schedule the meeting based on that input. No in-box filled with e-mails you need to sift through in order to determine the best date and time. You don't even need to create an account to use Doodle and there's no software that needs to be installed. What could be simpler?

Dropbox (www.dropbox.com)

Dropbox is a way to share files and folders with people. It's also a storage location, so you can readily access your own files and folders, no matter which computer or device you're using. Have you ever been working on a PowerPoint presentation that you wanted to share with a collaborator only to discover that the file is too large to send via e-mail? Dropbox to the rescue! There's a free version and you can pay to have more storage space.

Google Drive (drive.google.com)

Google Drive is not a time management tool per se but is such a useful tool for collaboration that I had to mention it here. With Google Drive, you can work together on documents or spreadsheets, even working with others on the document together in real-time. No software needs to be downloaded to your computer; you just need access to the web. Even if not using Google Drive for collaboration, it's useful for anyone who works on different computers throughout the day.

Basecamp (www.basecamp.com)

If you are searching for a complete project management tool, then Basecamp is a popular option you may want to check out. It includes to-do lists, file sharing and more. It is not free, but there is a 60-day free trial if you want to get a feel for it.

While these are great tools (and there are many others), your organization may already be using tools that could be adapted to the needs of your collaboration. Something as simple as a shared folder in a shared drive may be adequate for your collaborative work. Remember, it's not about finding the perfect tool. It is most important to be intentional and to openly communicate about shared goals and ways of achieving those goals.

CHAPTER 8 KEY TAKEAWAYS

- Most of the work you do is collaborative.
- Many time management strategies that work for an individual can be adopted for use by a group, too.
- Successful collaborations require shared objectives and timelines and thorough communication about tasks and responsibilities.
- Technology can assist with collaborative time and task management. Either use the features within the tools already being used by your organization or explore tools like Doodle and Dropbox to identify solutions for your collaborative work needs.

In this chapter, collaboration and its impact on time management have been discussed. Strategies and tools that can help you make the most of collaborative work have been highlighted. In the next chapter, the focus will continue to be on time management and others, as you read about ways to help other people effectively manage their time.

CHAPTER 9

Helping Others with Time Management

As a supervisor, director, mentor, or even peer, you may have opportunities to help others with time management, too. This may become a necessity over time as you and your colleagues begin more and more collaborative and group activities, and they seem unable to schedule time to work with you. Even if you are in a small library with little staff, the way that others are managing their time will impact you and it is important that time should be thoughtfully structured.

As previously mentioned, time management approaches are very individual and personal. The specific techniques and tools that work for you, may not work well for someone else. However, there are things you can do to help someone who is struggling with accomplishing goals and completing tasks. All of things included in this book as strategies for you to try on your own, could be helpful suggestions to share with others. Working with someone who doesn't seem to know where his or her time goes? Share strategies from Chapter 2 on time tracking. Think someone is struggling to find clarity around his or her priorities? Suggest techniques from Chapter 3. See someone struggling with procrastination and maybe even perfectionism? See if you can gracefully mention tips or examples from Chapters 5 or 6. Your approach to helping others with time management depends upon your role in the organization. If you are a manager, then helping others with their time management is a natural fit as part of the feedback and guidance you naturally provide. Managers can help their staff perform as efficiently and effectively as possible. In that case, providing training in time management is your best solution. As a manager or mentor, you can help provide realistic assessments regarding how long something will take.

If you are not a manager, but are a colleague working with others to carry out a project, then your suggestions will need to be framed appropriately. Asking others about their preferred time management and collaboration strategies is a great way to start the conversation.

For those who are working on a project, time management issues may come up during the project, and the resolution of those issues may affect the entire group and the outcome of the group's work. Someone's time management issues could certainly slow down the entire group's process. If that is the case, here is a list of things you can do.

1. **Talk about it.**

Don't let missed deadlines or ongoing procrastination be "white elephants" that no one dares to discuss. People often provide opportunities for us to easily start a conversation about time management. If someone says, "I feel like I have too much to do" or "I'm late with my time sheet again," that's a great opportunity to introduce *Crash Course in Time Management for Library Staff*. You need only say, "I have been reading this book about time management and it includes some good ideas that I have been trying out." Making it clear that time management is something that everyone can work on is a great way to start a meaningful conversation, which can lead to sharing strategies. Share the Table of Contents so they can see the various solutions to their dilemmas.

2. **Emphasize that time management can be learned.**

Suggest that time management is not an innate skill but instead is something that can be learned. For some, effective time management seems to happen more naturally. However, it really is something that everyone can improve.

If you are in a group planning or working on a project and one member makes a comment such as, "I need to not be such a perfectionist!" or "I was trying hard not to procrastinate on this," you can share Chapter 5 and help them get past procrastination. If a member of the group seems to be rushing at the last minute, you can ask if they have been distracted and that's an opportunity to follow-up with some concrete suggestions. This is a better approach than just nodding your head. You can demonstrate how to identify priorities by emphasizing the importance of setting goals, as discussed in Chapter 3, to help avoid procrastination or perfectionist tendencies on your upcoming project. Provide concrete tips and check-in with the individual at a later date to see how they are doing.

3. **Help break large projects down into smaller tasks.**

    When tasked with a large project, it's natural to feel some trepidation. It's important, however, not to let that apprehension stall work and progress. Especially if you are working with someone who has less experience working on large projects, it may be useful to talk about how to make the project more manageable and less intimidating. Look at the big picture and then determine the parts. Think about the logical order in which things will need to be completed. Provide encouragement and emphasize the importance of moving ahead. If someone is planning a big public program for the first time, for example, help them work backward from the program date to establish the tasks that will need to be completed to help make that event a success.

4. **Set deadlines and check-in dates for projects.**

    If you are working on a project with someone or are supervising someone who is working on a project, you may want to set deadlines or at least check in with others about deadlines they may have set. In addition to establishing a final deadline, also set check-in points along the way. These dates and times can help ensure steady and regular work toward a goal, rather than procrastinating until a final deadline looms near.

5. **Assist with time estimates.**

    If you are someone who is new to a job or a role, it can be challenging to make accurate estimates regarding how long tasks will take. Talking to someone who is experienced in completing the relevant tasks is a great way to get a feel for how long things will take. Putting together the agenda for a meeting can take 15 minutes if it's a task you have done many times before and if it's a group that regularly meets. Alternately, if you have never created a meeting agenda and you're working with a new group, then creating the agenda can take an hour or more. In a collaborative work environment, there are often factors that are beyond the control of one person and it's important to build cushions into timelines that acknowledge likely pauses, while waiting on responses from others.

6. **Help others realize when tasks need to be delegated.**

    Students working on group projects often sigh, "This would be so much easier if I could just do it myself." Sharing the workload does create challenges; however, it is a necessary thing in most libraries and on most projects. Collaboration can lead to more effective problem-solving, is necessary for shared workloads, and provides multiple perspectives, which can enhance the quality of a project or solution. Think of the old adage, "Two heads are better than one." Open communication about expectations and roles will help communication go more smoothly. A team that has worked together for a while will learn to build on the strengths of various team members. When one team member is taking on too much, however, it's important to emphasize the need to delegate and share the workload.

7. **Identify items that are higher priorities (and tasks that are lower priorities, too).**

People working in libraries have numerous things they could be working on during a particular day. Effective time management includes identifying which things are the highest priority, and therefore should receive your attention at that time. It also depends upon the personality of the different persons. This does not mean that one personality is better than another, but the personality defines how they must make use of time management.

Some people naturally see "the forest" and others see "a tree" in front of them. John is a "forest" person. He sees the entire forest, the big picture related to the total job. When John is paired with a tree person with whom he collaborates effectively, project planning moves steadily forward with sequenced steps and a time line to finish.

Sarah is somewhere in between. She may have a sense of the big picture, but she can also be easily distracted and needs to be kept on track, often being assigned to do tasks in her office with the door closed. As discussed in previous chapters, task management is something that can be learned, so helping Sarah develop that ability, while making the most of her ability to see the big picture, will help her succeed.

Callie, for example, is a "tree" person. She is very detail oriented and precise. In her technology-related role, these character traits are a great fit. She dives into problems and sticks with them until they are solved. Sometimes, however, she gets so focused on one task, that she neglects other tasks that also need to be completed. Her manager addresses this challenge by having weekly check-ins, during which they work together to identify the priorities for the week. As a manager, or as a person in the group who sees "the forest," you may sometimes need to help Callie and others like her to see the big picture in order to help identify priority tasks.

8. **Share tools and techniques, such as time logs or task lists.**

The right tool or technique can have a major impact on an individual's ability to effectively manage their time. If you see someone struggling to find time to complete all of the things they want or need to complete, consider letting them know about time logs shown in Chapter 4 and how they can help identify how someone is spending their time. If tasks seem to regularly fall off of someone's radar, suggest an app that you have used for task management or to-do lists (perhaps Evernote or Google Tasks) or just share a Post-it note strategy that has worked for you. Time management is something everyone is likely trying to do, so sharing tips and tools can help. Again, time management tip sharing should always be gracefully done in the spirit of "here's something I've tried."

CHAPTER 9 KEY TAKEAWAYS

- Strategies included in this book for you to try on your own could be helpful suggestions to share with others, too.
- Talking about time management is a way to understand the challenges others are experiencing and can provide an opportunity to share tips and strategies from this book or from your own experience.
- Struggling with time management isn't a personal shortcoming; it's a skill and awareness gap that you can help others overcome.

In this chapter, you've learned strategies for sharing what you have learned about time management from this book and through your own experiences. In the next chapter, you will pull it all together, creating a personal plan for time management that will not only serve your present needs but will help you prepare for and adapt to inevitable changes that are ahead.

CHAPTER 10

Your Personal Plan

As you read the final chapter of this book, it is time to move beyond an exploration of the broad range of time management topics and possibilities to select and create a concrete and actionable plan for yourself. Think back over the things you have read and the activities you have completed while working through this book. In Chapter 2, you tracked your time usage, perhaps discovering things that you didn't know. Then you learned about to-do lists and task management, covering both digital and analog options. Suggested techniques for focus and organization were shared, including highlights from the Pomodoro Technique and David Allen's *Getting Things Done* method, too. The importance of aligning how you spend your time with your goals and priorities was introduced. Obstacles to effective time management were summarized and you may have recognized yourself or your challenges in those descriptions. And finally, recognizing that you don't work in isolation, time management and collaboration was considered, with ideas for sharing time management techniques with others as appropriate.

Don't let anyone tell you that there is one right way to manage your time. Your style and your circumstances are unique and the time management strategy that works for you will be unique, too. While there is a great deal to be learned by reading books and articles written by others and by having conversations with others about their time management strategies, you will need to shape your own approach based on trial and error and personal knowledge. Both your professional time and your personal time management may require new solutions and strategies at some point.

CREATING YOUR PERSONAL APPROACH

Confession: I carry and use a paper daily planner. I would hate to lose it. I keep my planners from year to year and that has been surprisingly useful. It melds my personal and professional lives in a way the digital calendars I use do not. In part, I don't have confidence that the technology tools of today will be around in a couple of years. And how difficult will it be to transfer old things forward?

When I was younger, I kept a diary. Now I keep paper calendars. My life is more than my tasks and meetings, but just having a record of my tasks and meetings is usually enough to spark the memories that matter.

On the other hand, I love online to-do lists. Again, I use them in conjunction with paper notes. One of my current favorite tools is Evernote. I also use Tomighty regularly. I find it handy when I'm struggling with focus. This book has introduced you to a variety of online tools, but if a paper solution works better for you, embrace that simplicity. These are the things that work well for me. Your system may look very different. Adapting suggestions is usually better than trying to fit yourself into someone else's pattern. The path to take to develop your personalized time management plan includes these five steps:

1. **Track and analyze your time usage.** You need to have an accurate understanding of how you are currently using your time both personally and professionally. Keeping a time log for a few days provides a snapshot view of how you spend your hours and days. Awareness leads to an ability to accurately estimate how long tasks will take. Your time log analysis may also help you identify the obstacles that you face. In Chapter 1, you may have used a paper time log to track your time or you may have tried an online tool like Toggl.

2. **Determine your priorities and set goals.** Rather than reacting to events and situations, an effective time manager exerts more control over the way he or she spends time. When analyzing the time logs created in step one, gaps between what you are doing and what you want to be doing will become apparent. Reflection and communication with mentors and supervisors can help you determine the things that are a priority for you—the ways in which you want to be spending your time. In this space, create a list with five or six goals that are a top priority for you.

Prioritize spending your time working toward those goals.

3. **Select time management tools and techniques.** How will you find the time you need to achieve the goals you set in step two? Basic tools like to-do lists, calendars, schedules, and timers can help you take control of your time-identifying action steps toward accomplishing your goals. Calendars and schedules help you structure the 24 hours and 7 days a week that we each have. To-do lists identify tasks that need to be completed. Timers can help you find periods for focused attention. For each of these tools, there are analog options and there are digital options, too. You don't want to spend so much time searching for the perfect tool that it becomes a distraction or a way to procrastinate working on tasks that need to be completed. However, spending some time thoughtfully developing the system that will enable your best performance is time well spent. In this space, describe the tools you use. Include your calendar, schedules, to-do lists, and timers. Also describe any tools that you would like to explore or research more completely.

4. Identify and address your personal time management obstacles. Whether you are a procrastinator, a perfectionist, or someone who deals with a lot of distractions and interruptions at work, there are steps you can take to overcome these obstacles. Believe that you can change and experiment with finding ways to do so. In this space, create a list of the obstacles that you are focused on addressing. Include not only the obstacle but also the strategies you will use.

5. Prepare for the time management challenges presented by collaboration. A great deal of the work many people in libraries do is collaborative. This makes it necessary to not only address your own time management strategies but also to address time management issues and challenges that are impacting your team. Many of the same techniques used by an individual can be adapted for use by a team.

CONTINUING TO LEARN AND GROW

Hopefully, reading this book has provided an opportunity to reflect about your current time management techniques and to explore and try new things. Remember that time management is *not* a gift that anyone is either born with or does not possess. It can be learned. There are many tools out there and you are encouraged to explore even beyond the tools that are mentioned in this book. Ask others about their favorite tools and techniques and give things a try.

Be careful not to get **too** enamored with trying out new tools. As one librarian joked:

I get too involved in finding the perfect tool and not involved enough in actually using them.

Some things you try now will stick and some will not. Just because you aren't still using a tool six months from now doesn't mean that it doesn't have value at this stage in your learning process. There's always a chance you'll find a tool or technique that you will still be using six years from now. You don't know until you try. You may find, like I did, that a combination of tools works best for you. Enjoy your exploration!

It takes a while to turn a new behavior into a habit. Give new techniques and tools a chance to take hold. Once something is a habit, as discussed in Chapter 4, using it becomes so routine that you don't have to think about it.

Developing your time management strategies is a continuous work in progress. Keep experimenting with techniques and investigating tools. You'll develop a flexible and evolving system that works best for your own needs. Be sure to talk to friends, family, and coworkers about their time management strategies. Participating in conversations about time management keeps us aware of our own habits, both good and bad. Remember the timeboxing technique shared in Chapter 4? Timebox 15 minutes every now and then to browse Lifehacker (www.lifehacker .com), a website focused on tips, tricks, and downloads for getting things done. The *Harvard Business Review* (www.hbr.org) is another great place to look for time management and productivity inspiration. If you are a parent and are focused on the special time management challenges that presents, Christine Carter's site (www.christinecarter.com) is a great place for inspiration and reassurance.

Once you become an effective time manager, using strategies and tools that may benefit others, consider sharing your successes with others. Seek out opportunities to promote time management, perhaps at staff meetings in your organization or at library conferences, too. You may be surprised to discover how receptive people are to ideas regarding improved time management.

As mentioned earlier in the book, it is not always you that needs to change and become more efficient. Sometimes your supervisors or library boards need to have more realistic expectations. They may not realize the extent of duties you are fulfilling and the constraints on your available time. There are times when a library's organizational structures need to adapt and change in order to best support the work of library employees. And on a larger scale, as you seek to get things done and remain sane while doing so, you sometimes realize that it is your society that could and should change to better support the needs of working individuals. Time off after the birth of child, mental health sabbaticals, and support for working at home are all examples of time management support that can make a big difference. These things are happening in some places and in your work to raise your own awareness about time management; you can perhaps raise awareness regarding what would be good for the many, too.

BIBLIOGRAPHY

Allen, David. *Getting Things Done: The Art of Stress-Free Productivity (revised edition)*. New York: Penguin Group USA, 2015.

Brown, Brené. *The Gifts of Imperfection: Let Go of Who You Think You're Supposed to Be and Embrace Who You Are*. Center City, MN: Hazelden Publishing, 2010.

Burka, Jane and Lenora Yuen. *Procrastination: Why You Do It, What To Do about It Now*. Cambridge, MA: Perseus Books Group, 2003.

Carter, Christine. *The Sweet Spot: How to Find Your Groove at Home and Work*. New York: Ballantine Books, 2015.

Collins, Jim. *Good to Great*. New York: Harper Collins, 2001.

Csikszentmihalyi, Mihaly. *Finding Flow: The Psychology of Engagement with Everyday Life*. New York: Perseus Books Group, 1997.

Duhigg, Charles. *The Power of Habit: Why We Do What We Do in Life and Business*. New York: Random House, 2014.

Hallowell, Ned. *Driven to Distraction at Work: How to Focus and Be More Productive*. Boston: Harvard Business School Publishing, 2015.

Szymanski, Jane. *The Perfectionist's Handbook: Take Risks, Invite Criticism, and Make the Most of Your Mistakes*. Hoboken, NJ: John Wiley and Sons, 2011.

Vanderkam, Laura. *I Know How She Does It: How Successful Women Make the Most of Their Time*. New York: Penguin Group USA, 2015.

Vanderkam, Laura. *168 Hours: You Have More Time Than You Think*. New York: Penguin Group USA, 2010.

INDEX

ABOUT THE AUTHOR

Brenda Hough has focused on professional development in libraries for more than 20 years. Her work in libraries has included assessments, evaluations, training, and instruction for national, state, and local initiatives as well as projects with Infopeople, the Bill and Melinda Gates Foundation, WebJunction, the Public Library Association, the Edge Initiative, and the Association of Specialized and Cooperative Library Agencies. Hough is committed to providing opportunities for library staff to expand their knowledge and skills so that they can best meet the needs of the communities they serve. Her website is www.brendahough.com.